ETHICS
IN THE
NEW
TESTAMENT

Jack T. Sanders

ETHICS
IN THE
NEW
TESTAMENT

Change and Development

FORTRESS PRESS   **Philadelphia**

Library of Congress Catalog Card Number 74–26342

ISBN 0–8006–0404–0

4692L74   Printed in U.S.A.   1–404

IN MEMORIAM
Patricia Chism Sanders
1936-1973
who taught me most of what I know
about love

CONTENTS

LIST OF ABBREVIATIONS

BZNW	Beihefte zur *ZNW*
CBQ	*Catholic Biblical Quarterly*
EvTh	*Evangelische Theologie*
FRLANT	Forschungen zur Religion und Literatur des Alten und Neuen Testaments
HarvTheolRev	*Harvard Theological Review*
HNT	Handbuch zum Neuen Testament
ICC	International Critical Commentary
JBL	*Journal of Biblical Literature*
JR	*Journal of Religion*
JThC	*Journal for Theology and the Church*
NTS	*New Testament Studies*
RevThom	*Revue Thomiste*
RSV	*Revised Standard Version of the Old Testament*
ScotJourTheol	*Scottish Journal of Theology*
SBT	Studies in Biblical Theology
ThLZ	*Theologische Literaturzeitung*
ThR	*Theologische Rundschau*
ZNW	*Zeitschrift für die neutestamentliche Wissenschaft*
ZThK	*Zeitschrift für Theologie und Kirche*

Two students on the porch of the student union. One is playing a mouth organ and the other dancing. I cannot put out of mind the impression of an organ grinder and his monkey. I pass by and go inside. When I come out, the two are still there, and the dancer is holding out a saucer with some small change in it to all passers-by. I drop in a quarter. "Bless you brother." I can spare the quarter; I start to cross the street. "You have three numbers coming." I look back and motion as if waving him away. "Right *on!*"

On my desk is a stack of appeals for donations. They are from charitable organizations and from political candidates and causes I believe in. I look through them, knowing that my BankAmericard balance is getting larger every month. I pick out one local charity and one candidate and throw the others away. Then I put the two envelopes aside for next month.

India has just invaded East Pakistan. My sympathies are with the Bengalis and against the (West) Pakistanis. I consider writing to my senators and congressman, urging them to press for U.S. foreign policy that favors the Bengalis; but they are all Republicans, and the Nixon administration is making the foreign policy. I decide instead to write a letter to the editor of my local newspaper.

These examples are placed here not to titillate the reader with glimpses into my personal life, but to underscore the issue which has prompted this study. That issue is the present crisis in ethics. Ethics is one of the most pressing problems of our time, and it will be the purpose of this work to investigate, in part, one aspect of the problem: the relation of the New Testament to ethics. Specifically, the question to be posed is whether and to what degree an Occidental of the modern day may look to the New Testament for any guidance or clues for behavior. The choice of the term "Occidental" rather than "Christian" is deliberate, since not only most Christians, but also many others who may be of another faith or not religious at all frequently refer to the "Judaeo-Christian ethic" or to "the ethic(s) of love" as some kind of generally valid ethical standard for the West and for Occidentals. It was, for example, reported in a local newspaper that a ranking member of the U.S. State Department some months ago suggested to Arab and Israeli diplomats that they might be more Christian in their attitudes. Such a story (which, admittedly, may be embellished or fanciful) serves to illustrate the fact that there is a widespread allegiance in the West to "Christian" ethical principles. Thus it is important to clarify what is involved in the ethical principles of the formative period of Christianity—that is, those that may be found in the various writings that make up the New Testament.

It will have to be realized that everyone lives in a highly complex ethical situation. This ethical situation requires both individual and corporate response, the two sometimes separate, sometimes overlapping, sometimes conflicting. Further, what we have come to call our "pluralistic society" confuses ethical issues to a still greater degree, especially on the corporate level, since the possibility is immediately raised that a "Christian" ethics may not be appropriate to such a society, being composed, as it is, of a variety of non-Christian groups and individuals. Because of this complex ethical situation, our inquiry regarding the New Testament will have to raise the question as to whether it may be, even in part, valid for individual ethics, corporate ethics, or both; and whether this validity may extend to a pluralistic society. To be sure, there is hardly any hope of finding specific instructions that will still be valid after nearly two thousand years, but whether the New Testament provides a general ethical validity—middle axioms, norms, or even a mere direction of response—that will be the question.

The discerning reader will doubtless miss, here and there, a reference to some work or other that might have been appropriate. I readily confess that I have not here referred to every significant work dealing with every book in the New Testament. To do so would have turned this work into a collection of footnotes and little else; but I trust that I have not overlooked any significant *position* that might have been relevant for a consideration of the subject matter. What does need to be mentioned here is that my indebtedness to two writers, Herbert Preisker and Rudolf Bultmann, probably exceeds what one would gather by noting the frequency with which their names occur herein.

Except for a few places where, for convenience, I have quoted from the Revised Standard Version of the Old Testament (Division of Christian Education of the National Council of the Churches of Christ in the United States of America, 1952), all translations of foreign language works cited herein—including the New Testament—are my own. Chapters 1 and 2 have previously appeared as articles in, respectively, *Journal of the American Academy of Religion* 38 (1970): 131–46, and *Biblical Research* 14 (1969): 19–32, and are here printed in rather revised form by permission.

Finally, I should like to offer a note of grateful thanks to Ms. Jean Nyland, who skillfully and patiently rendered an extremely difficult draft into an excellent typescript, and to Linda Richman, who did most of the preparation of the indexes.

I

JESUS

A considerable number of Christian theologians (including pastors and theological students) assume and will argue that Jesus left an ethical *teaching* which all Christians should attempt to follow. An example of this view is to be found in the *Interpreter's Dictionary of the Bible,* where it is stated that the Golden Rule (Matt. 7:12) is "a climactic summary of the Sermon on the Mount," and that this, along with the commandment to love God and one's neighbor as oneself, "justifies the conclusion that love *(agapē)* was of the essence of Jesus' ethical teaching." The discussion of Jesus' ethical teaching is then concluded with the affirmation that "the ethics of Jesus is best thought of as the demands which are placed upon those who have accepted God's rule, as Jesus proclaimed and lived it."[1] Yet such a position is not without problems.

ETHICS AND ESCHATOLOGY—The Problem

One always runs a risk in finding in Jesus, in his teachings or his life, a guide for ethics in one's own day. This risk is what Henry Cadbury, at the height of the Social Gospel period, labeled "the peril of modernizing Jesus." Discussing particularly "Limitations of Jesus' Social Teaching,"[2] Cadbury effectively argued that Jesus' teaching was totally lacking in the grounds needed to derive a social ethics from it. "Nowhere," he stated, "do I find unmistakable appeal to the rights or needs of the other party or even to the interests of society in general."[3] He found Jesus to be concerned with the *being of the individual addressed*—as with the one

1. W. D. Davies, "Ethics in the NT," in *Interpreter's Dictionary of the Bible,* vol. 2 (New York and Nashville, 1962), pp. 168, 172.
2. Henry J. Cadbury, *The Peril of Modernizing Jesus,* pp. 86–119.
3. Ibid., p. 102.

(Luke 10) who was supposed to *be* a neighbor—and not with "the recipient of social service."[4] In refuting any example of what he called the "social misunderstanding of Jesus," Cadbury warned the generation between the wars, "We must be particularly careful not to quote him as the ally and prophet of our modern social programs and reforms. There may be reasons for a modern Christian to espouse prohibition, pacifism, socialism or communism as so many liberal Christians do. But to claim Jesus as holding in any explicit, literal or conscious way such modern philosophies is the grossest anachronism." To this he added, "Of course by the same token the capitalists and militarists have no more right to claim him."[5]

Cadbury consciously avoided arguing from *konsequente Eschatologie* ("thoroughgoing" or, in Cadbury's more accurate English, "consistent eschatology"). He thought that this view might not win the day—as indeed it did not—and that it was better to argue from specific texts, i.e., that a certain saying of Jesus could not have meant what those appropriating it on behalf of the social gospel took it to mean. (For this purpose, Cadbury also found it expedient to accept most such sayings of Jesus as authentic.)

To argue from the individual sayings, however, is precarious, for the possibility always exists that one may have misinterpreted a saying, or that both sides may have overlooked a significant saying; or Jesus may be modernized in some other way, and then one must go through all the material again. Ultimately, any such argument against "modernizing" Jesus can be conclusive only when it deals with the foundation of his teachings—that is, with his basic religious orientation. It was in fact thoroughgoing eschatology that had done this.

In his justly famous book, *The Quest of the Historical Jesus,* subtitled, "A Critical Study of Its Progress from Reimarus to Wrede," Albert Schweitzer had sought to show the general invalidity of modernizing Jesus' teachings. The reason for this invalidity was that Jesus of Nazareth shared with many of his contemporaries a fundamentally eschatological outlook and that this way of perceiving reality, which does not permit of transposi-

4. Ibid., p. 110.
5. Ibid., p. 112.

tion into the modern world, conditioned all Jesus' teachings, especially his ethical teachings. "As a water-plant is beautiful so long as it is growing in the water," wrote Schweitzer, "but once torn from its roots, withers and becomes unrecognisable, so it is with the historical Jesus when He is wrenched loose from the soil of eschatology, and the attempt is made to conceive Him 'historically' as a Being not subject to temporal conditions."[6] Specifically regarding Jesus' ethical teachings, this means that Jesus' ethical outlook was conditioned by his eschatological outlook. That is true even for the oft quoted Sermon on the Mount. "Only the phrase, 'Repent for the Kingdom of God is at hand' and its variants belong to the public preaching. And this, therefore, is the only message which He commits to His disciples when sending them forth. What this repentance, supplementary to the law, the special ethic of the interval before the coming of the Kingdom (*Interimsethik*) is, in its positive acceptation, He explains in the Sermon on the Mount."[7]

Schweitzer made it clear that Jesus intended only, in his opinion, an interim ethics. "There is for Jesus no ethic of the Kingdom of God, for in the Kingdom of God all natural relationships . . . are abolished. Temptation and sin no longer exist. . . . To serve, to humble oneself, to incur persecution and death, belong to the 'ethic of the interim' just as much as does penitence."[8] This view that Jesus' ministry was primarily determined by his imminent eschatology (an insight which Schweitzer, to be sure, inherited and expanded upon) has found quite a large following among New Testament scholars, although presumably no one today accepts his analysis of the eschatological historicity of Mark. There have been, of course, those who have rejected such a view of Jesus' ministry. Among the most prominent of such "dissenters" from the eschatological consensus has been C. H. Dodd, whose "realized eschatology" is presented most clearly in his book, *The Parables of the Kingdom*. It was Dodd's position that "Jesus intended to proclaim the Kingdom of God not as something to

6. Albert Schweitzer, *The Quest of the Historical Jesus*, p. 399.
7. Ibid., p. 352; cf. further the posthumously published *The Kingdom of God and Primitive Christianity*, pp. 93 f.
8. Schweitzer, *Quest of the Historical Jesus*, p. 364.

come in the near future, but as a matter of present experience."[9]

Among New Testament scholars of the present generation, apocalyptic has come in for considerable discussion,[10] and, from two different quarters within this discussion, the view that Jesus held an imminent eschatology has received a more thoroughgoing onslaught than that of Dodd. Ernst Käsemann has sought to explain Jesus' position as one which finds its beginning in the preaching of John the Baptist but which then rejects the apocalyptic aspect of that proclamation, so that

> . . . only the *basileia* sayings which go back to Jesus himself remain uncontested. It can hardly be disputed that God's lordship is for the most part regarded in them as yet to come into force. Characteristically, however, the way in which this is expressed in the more certainly authentic material does not emphasize the apocalyptic element very strongly.[11]

This is then what marks the difference between Jesus and John. Käsemann argues that Jesus' "own preaching . . . did not bear a fundamentally apocalyptic stamp but proclaimed the immediacy of the God who was near at hand." After Jesus, the church turned again to the apocalyptic views he had played down, and apocalyptic became "the mother of all Christian theology."[12]

9. C. H. Dodd, *The Parables of the Kingdom*, p. 31. Cf. also Heinz-Dietrich Wendland, *Ethik des Neuen Testaments*, p. 29, who argues that Jesus' ethical demands can be carried out because "the overlordship of evil is broken. . . . the will of God can be done" because of the presence of the Kingdom.

10. It would serve little purpose to attempt to give here a full bibliography of that discussion, but the reader is referred especially to the articles appearing in *JThC* 6 (1969), a volume devoted entirely to the subject and titled *Apocalypticism*; and to an article by Jean Carmignac, "Les dangers de l'eschatologie," *NTS* 17 (1971): 365–90, which especially discusses the difference between "eschatology" and "apocalyptic."

11. Ernst Käsemann, "On the Subject of Primitive Christian Apocalyptic," *New Testament Questions of Today*, p. 111. Probably the most extensive recent work to attempt again a reconstruction of an authentic corpus of Jesus' sayings is Norman Perrin's *Rediscovering the Teaching of Jesus*. After an analysis of a number of future oriented sayings and parables, including the Son of man sayings, Perrin concludes (pp. 202–6) that Jesus emphasized not the future but present immediacy and the promise of a future qualitatively related to the emphasis on present immediacy. Quite similarly to Käsemann, Perrin states that "the only elements which go back to Jesus here are such general things as the expectation of vindication and judgment implied by the parables" (p. 203). From such a conclusion, however, the further conclusion necessarily follows that Jesus shared with John the Baptist an imminent eschatology. If he did not consider God's vindication and judgment *pressing*, i.e., *near at hand*, then the parables make no sense.

12. Käsemann, "The Beginnings of Christian Theology," *New Testament Questions of Today*, pp. 101 f.

From a quite different angle of approach (an analysis of the parables of Jesus, not a description of the development of early Christian theology), Robert W. Funk has reached a similar position, although one that goes farther than Käsemann's in rejecting imminence. Funk's study of the form and function of the parables has led him to define them as "pieces of everydayness [that] have an unexpected 'turn' in them which looks through the common-place" not to the coming Kingdom of God, but "to a new view of reality."[13] Another way of putting this is to say that the parable "is the linguistic aperture onto a world qualified by something other than the anonymous 'they.' . . . In the parable [Jesus] raises a new world into being, so to speak, out of the linguistic debris of the old."[14] Thus, whereas Käsemann still wished to speak of the "immediacy of the God who was near at hand" and of the imme-diacy of his Kingdom in the message of Jesus (a position which is, to this degree, identical with that of Schweitzer), while relegating any apocalyptic coloration in that message to the early church, Funk goes so far as to reject even the language of imminent ex-pectation and to speak of another world which may be glimpsed if one enters the logic of the parable.[15]

Any view, however, which holds that Jesus did not proclaim an imminent eschatology, i.e., did not preach that the Kingdom of God was about to come, was even in the process of dawning, misses an essential point. That Jesus held an imminent escha-tology will have to be considered a fact. This is most clearly seen in his endorsement of the ministry of John the Baptist (Matt. 11:7–11a, 16–19 par.), an endorsement that is surely to be viewed as authentic in view of the fact that it proved an embarrassment

---

13. Robert W. Funk, *Language, Hermeneutic, and Word of God*, p. 161.
14. Ibid., p. 196.
15. In his article, "The Looking-Glass Tree Is for the Birds," *Interpretation* 27 (1973): 8, Funk has divorced Jesus' concept of the Kingdom of God altogether from future expectation when he refers to "what the Kingdom really is, namely, the faith to dwell in the Kingdom." He is therefore more consistent than Käsemann, who is in the somewhat embarrassing position of saying that Jesus maintained imminent eschatology but rejected apocalyptic and that after Jesus apocalyptic became again attached to his imminent eschatology. Apparently, Jesus was not clear enough as a teacher to explain the difference to his followers! Or perhaps the disciples were clods, which is also a possibility. One should note that Funk has rejected temporal language in favor of spatial, a not uncommon occurrence in the history of Christianity.

to the church, as Matt. 11:11b, a Christian attempt to alter the
first saying, attests.[16] The saying found in Matt. 11:12 f., the more
original form of which is probably maintained in Luke 16:16
(entering the Kingdom violently), probably also signifies the imminence involved in Jesus' proclamation of the Kingdom, although the exact meaning of this logion is uncertain. Clearer,
however, are the parable of the fig tree (Mark 13:28 f.), which
implies that God's eschatological summer, i.e., the Kingdom of
God is near; and the saying about seeing Satan falling like lightning (Luke 10:18).[17] Finally, a number of sayings about "entering
the Kingdom" will almost certainly be authentic sayings of Jesus,
even if the early church could (e.g., Matt. 5:20; 7:21) make use of
this phrase for its own purposes. These are Mark 9:43–47; 10:15;
Matt. 21:31b; Luke 11:52. Thus, on this evidence alone, any view
which does not treat Jesus as espousing a view of imminent eschatology will have to be considered self-apocopating.

Funk, in fact, appears to have overlooked the way in which
Jesus' expectation of the imminent coming of God's Kingdom has
affected the parables, has colored the new world to which the
parables point. This may be seen in the parable of the good
Samaritan, the second of the two parables analyzed extensively in
Funk's book. Funk is correct in rejecting designating the parable
a *Beispielerzählung* (exemplary story),[18] and one can agree with
his conclusion that "the parable is an invitation to comport one-

16. Richard H. Hiers, *The Kingdom of God in the Synoptic Tradition*, pp. 62–65,
takes the whole verse to be authentic and those "in the Kingdom" to be angels; the
saying thus means that "the final time *before* the coming of the Kingdom of God
has come" (p. 64). Why the saying would thus take on such a temporal orientation
is altogether unclear; I regard a reference to angels as farfetched. A much better
explanation of the verse has been offered by M. Jack Suggs, *Wisdom, Christology,
and Law in Matthew's Gospel* (Cambridge, Mass., 1970), p. 47, in reliance on Oscar
Cullmann, "The Significance of the Qumran Texts for Research into the Beginnings
of Christianity," *JBL* 74 (1955): 219. Suggs points out that *mikroteros* in v. 11b
should properly be translated "lesser" instead of "least," and that the clause therefore refers to Jesus, who started out as a disciple of the Baptist, therefore the
"lesser" of the two. Suggs does not discuss the question of authenticity.

17. Hiers, *Kingdom of God*, p. 56, concludes, after an analysis of the last saying,
that it means that "Satan's power is being overcome," not that Satan has already
been defeated. That is correct.

18. Funk, *Language, Hermeneutic, and Word of God*, p. 211. As a matter of fact,
the parable originally had nothing to do with the love commandment. This has
now been thoroughly demonstrated by John Dominic Crossan, "Parable and Example in the Teaching of Jesus," *NTS* 18 (1972): 285–96. It is rather a parable of the
manner of the inbreaking of the Kingdom of God (ibid., p. 295). Unfortunately,
Crossan takes the parable to be *also* an exemplary story.

self with reality in the way the Samaritan does."[19] It is with Funk's definition of that reality, however, that one must quarrel, for he has overlooked an essential ingredient. The reality, the world into which the hearer (reader) of the parable is invited, may be stated in this way: "The reign of God is as near as the parable, in which it may provisionally arrive. The parable thus forges an eschatological unity of promise and demand."[20] Correctly put, if by that Funk means that the behavior described in the parable makes sense only if the God who vindicates the righteous is about to come; but that is not what Funk means. He holds firmly on to his atemporal understanding of Kingdom and refers to "the occasion for love to come into play."[21] But the parable of the good Samaritan does more than merely open up for the hearer (reader) the possibility that love may come into play. It says more about the Kingdom than that it lies just on the horizon of our vision, discernible if we only direct our attention toward it, ever ready to be appropriated as our world, as my world, even if only temporarily. If we agree that the parable does in fact define (in some way adequately for Jesus) the Kingdom of God as love, then it behooves us to look very carefully at the definition. If we are invited "to comport [ourselves] with reality in the way the Samaritan does," then we must be certain of that way. Here is where, it seems to me, Funk has failed to take everything into account, for he has nowhere noted the way in which the Samaritan's acts of love escalate.

This escalation in the parable is what provides the truly shocking element. If the hearer is startled by the advent of the Samaritan, he is knocked off his feet by what the Samaritan does; for this intruding and therefore attention getting element (the Samaritan) *proceeds to behave as no man ever behaved!*[22] Not only does

19. Ibid., p. 216.
20. Ibid., p. 220.
21. Ibid., p. 221.
22. Hendrikus Boers, *Theology Out of the Ghetto: A New Testament Exegetical Study Concerning Religious Exclusiveness* (Leiden; 1971), pp. 22–5, proposes just the opposite, i.e., that the parable of the good Samaritan accurately described the world of the hearers, and that Jesus gained authority by the keen accuracy of the description. This explanation is proposed as an alternate to the view that the parable must be true because it possesses the authority of Jesus, even if it does not agree with the perceived world of the hearers. Although I am in sympathy with Boers's attempt to rescue New Testament material from the trappings of a priori

he stop to render aid, but he provides ambulance service; not only does he provide ambulance service, but he remains at the hospital overnight as attending physician and nurse; not only does he offer special medical care, but he tenders up his Blue Cross card (or his bank account, take your choice) as guarantee of payment for all further hospital bills for the injured man, *however extensive they may be*. And then he rides off into the west! Here indeed is an adequate description of *agapē*; and here indeed is eschatological promise. Funk is correct in that. But how can this parable forge "an eschatological unity of promise and *demand*" (italics mine)? How can I be demanded to behave as no man ever behaved, to behave in what has to be labeled an *impossible* way? He who truly understands what *agapē* means for Jesus and Paul understands that it is everything that man is not. Karl Barth correctly came to that conclusion in his discussion of 1 Cor. 13.[23] Funk's "eschatological unity of promise and demand" has touched the right chord, but Funk has explained away the truly startling aspect of the parable by understanding eschatological to mean "possible" rather than "impossible."

Put another way, the parable does intend to explain the Samaritan's comportment as possible, but one must be clear on what terms, under what circumstances. The Samaritan's comportment cannot be possible to every man who, at any time, sees as the Samaritan sees; it cannot be possible to the one who, by his own choosing, decides to step into the Samaritan's world. The most characteristic aspect of the Samaritan's behavior is that it is not of this world! He who enters the Samaritan's world of comportment toward his fellow man of necessity leaves the (how can it be phrased otherwise?) present world; for where are the Samaritan's family and employment, whence come his unlimited leisure and unlimited funds? Funk's choice of terms is apt: the Samaritan is

---

authority with which the church has invested it, I have to say that he has completely missed the point of this parable. It does not present a world familiar to the hearers. Funk is, rather, correct; it points to another world on the horizon. Whereas Funk sees the eschatological orientation of the parable, although he turns the temporal transcendence into spatial, Boers has collapsed the difference into immanence and has thereby misconstrued the parable.

23. Karl Barth, *The Resurrection of the Dead*, p. 85. On this point, cf. further below, in the chapter on Paul; and my earlier article, "First Corinthians 13: Its Interpretation Since the First World War," *Interpretation* 20 (1966): 159–87.

in another world, a world in which they do not marry nor are they given in marriage, a world in which men leave their nets and become fishers of men, a world in which one serves God alone and unrighteous Mammon not at all. This world has a well-known name, and that is the Kingdom of God. The Kingdom of God, however, is not a world that remains ever on the horizon, waiting for mortals to flit, as it were, in and out; for to enter the world that is the Kingdom of God is to cut off all ties with the present world. It is to forsake family, to leave the dead to bury the dead; and the one who, having put his hand to the plow, even *looks back* does not belong in it.

Under what circumstances, then, is the Samaritan's comportment possible to the hearer (reader) of the parable? It is plain to the hearer that to accept the demand of the parable is to accept an eschatological reality: the imminent arrival of the Kingdom of the God who vindicates the righteous. That is the only hope of the one who accepts the demand of the parable; for the one who accepts the demand of the parable is destined to leave this world one way or another. If the righteous God does not come shortly, the one who accepts the demand of the parable will either starve to death or wind up a derelict. The only circumstance under which the Samaritan's "comportment with reality" becomes a possibility is a belief in God's coming Kingdom and a belief, in fact, that the Kingdom is coming so soon that one stands to gain by living as if it were already present.[24]

If imminent eschatology cannot be rooted out of the message of Jesus, a third alternative therefore immediately suggests itself; that is the possibility that, although Jesus did expect the Kingdom of God to come soon, his significance for ethics may endure beyond the disappointing of that expectation. Such a possibility has been offered by Amos Wilder in his book, *Eschatology and Ethics in the Teaching of Jesus*. In this work, Wilder quite readily accepts not only Jesus' eschatological orientation, but also the fact

---

24. I find it puzzling in the extreme that Victor Paul Furnish, *The Love Command in the New Testament*, pp. 67 f., notes *that* "in Jesus' teaching the love command is set fully within the context of the eschatological proclamation about the coming Rule of God," but he makes *no attempt whatever to explain what that proclamation was or to explain how the proclamation was related to the love commandment.* He seems to find eschatology and ethics, in Jesus' proclamation, juxtaposed but unrelated.

that the imminent eschatology provided, by its emphasis on "reward and penalty," "sanctions" for Jesus' ethics.[25] Such eschatologically oriented sanctions, however, he considers to have been
only "formal" sanctions, the "fundamental sanctions" being given
by Jesus' proclamation of the "nature of God" and his appeal to
the scriptures and by the "authority and example of Jesus."[26]

Problems with this position begin, however, when Wilder attempts to keep the eschatology as a constitutive element of Jesus'
teaching. He writes,

> We do not wish to rule out entirely the place of such sanction in the
> teaching. He would be foolish who would try to do so in the face of
> the Judgment parables and pointed summons to vigilance. Even read
> as dramatizations such passages definitely bring into play, and legiti-
> mately, the self-regarding motives as over against the future. But
> these formal sanctions should be looked upon as supplementary
> rather than as compromising the fundamental sanctions.[27]

What is problematical in this statement is the supposition that
the eschatology is related to the ethics only in terms of future reward and punishment. That is really not to understand the role
of imminence in Jesus' thinking. The Jesus who called John the
Baptist the greatest man on earth (Matt. 11:11a) and who saw
"Satan falling like lightning from heaven" (Luke 10:18) was convinced that God's final action in world history was beginning.
Hence, in agreement with the Baptist, he saw the present moment
as the final moment for repentance. Indeed, it is correctly observed by Wilder that repentance was necessary in the face of
God's righteousness, but that is because God's righteousness was
considered to be *at hand*. It is an academic question to ask, as
Wilder apparently does, what ethics Jesus might have taught if he

25. Amos N. Wilder, *Eschatology and Ethics in the Teaching of Jesus*, pp. 73–115.
A much less satisfactory attempt than Wilder's to show the continuing relevance of
Jesus' ethics in spite of his eschatology is that of Wendland, who notes *(Ethik des
Neuen Testaments*, p. 31) the unity of "eschatological proclamation" and "ethical
demand" for Jesus, but who then proceeds (p. 32) to argue that Jesus' ethics,
because of its "interim" character, calls the present age into question.
26. Wilder, *Eschatology and Ethics*, pp. 116–32.
27. Ibid., p. 141. The same line of argument is also followed by Hans Conzelmann,
An Outline of the Theology of the New Testament, pp. 117 f. and p. 125. Conzelmann attempts to distinguish (p. 118) between Jesus' call to repentance, based on
the coming Kingdom of God, and Jesus' specific ethical demands, especially the love
commandment, based on "the example and will of God." The same criticisms apply
here as to Wilder's argument.

had not agreed emphatically with the Baptist that the end was imminent. The true historical question regarding Jesus' ethics must be answered precisely as Albert Schweitzer answered it,[28] i.e., that Jesus' imminent expectation prompted his ethical teaching, and that the ethics cannot be discussed apart from the eschatology.

In the last analysis, if God's righteousness is the basic reality behind the call to righteousness, must not God's judgment also be included within the horizon of the "fundamental sanctions"? If judgment is thus inseparably connected, as it seems, with divine righteousness, then the eschatology has to be retained and cannot ultimately be overcome by Wilder's reconstruction. This being the case, we may now turn to an examination of views—in the development of theology following Schweitzer—in which imminent eschatology is seen to be constitutive for Jesus, while at the same time an ethical significance or validity is asserted for Jesus.

THE BULTMANNIAN SOLUTION

In his book on Jesus,[29] Rudolf Bultmann apparently attempted to hold on to the two alternatives for understanding Jesus that Schweitzer had so clearly delineated. That is to say, Bultmann recognized as well as anyone else Jesus' apocalyptic orientation but nevertheless sought relevance in his teachings. Of course, Bultmann later wrote, "*The message of Jesus* is a presupposition for the theology of the New Testament rather than a part of that theology itself."[30] Here, however, he states equally plainly that "the investigation concerns the content, meaning, and validity for us of what is taught in the gospels."[31] This is of course a famous problem in Bultmann's system, but it is of no purpose to attempt to resolve it here; rather, the question to be asked is whether Bultmann's Jesus book has provided any justification for considering Jesus' teachings to be relevant for modern ethics. Bultmann at first seems to deny any such significance by affirming that

28. To be sure, without agreeing in detail with Schweitzer's reconstruction, as was already indicated above.
29. Rudolf Bultmann, *Jesus and the Word.*
30. Rudolf Bultmann, *Theology of the New Testament*, vol. 1, p. 3.
31. Bultmann, *Jesus and the Word*, p. 123.

"Jesus teaches no ethics at all in the sense of an intelligible theory valid for all men." Such a theory would have to presuppose an anthropology, and would make man "the measure of human action."[32] Jesus calls instead for a radical obedience to God's will,[33] and Bultmann clearly understands this to imply a contextual ethics.

> This moment of decision contains all that is necessary for the decision, since in it the whole of life is at stake. . . . The crisis of decision is the situation in which all observation is excluded, for which *Now* alone has meaning, which is absorbed wholly in the present moment. *Now* must man know what to do and leave undone, and no standard whatsoever from the past or from the universal is available.[34]

Love (*agapē*) may be another way of expressing the radicality of this existential contextualism,[35] yet Bultmann rejects the notion that *agapē* can "be regarded as an ethical principle from which particular concrete requirements can be derived."[36] It would never be possible to say, "Because I love, I must do such and such"—neither in advance of a situation, nor in the situation itself. As Bultmann understands Jesus' command to love, it would be impossible ever to calculate from love to action; *agapē* rather means doing what *must* be done *now*—that is, letting the context provide even what must substitute for norms.

Bultmann was of course employing *Sachkritik* here (a critical analysis that seeks the true subject matter), just as he saw Jesus to have made use of *Sachkritik* with respect to the Jewish law.[37] There can be no doubt that Jesus himself would be surprised to see what was in his mind probably a purifying of that law in prospect of the dawning Kingdom cast in such existential terms. Yet some of his radical commands surely in fact imply that which Bultmann has explicated. Can the modern person, then, appeal to Jesus for a contextualism valid for today? The problem, unfortunately, lies again in the eschatological orientation, just as

32. Ibid., pp. 84 f.
33. Ibid., passim, particularly pp. 64–84.
34. Ibid., pp. 87 f.
35. Ibid., pp. 110 f.
36. Ibid., p. 112.
37. Cf. the discussion of Jesus' sovereignty over against the law based on his understanding of the true content and purpose of the law, ibid., p. 75.

Albert Schweitzer made clear; for, as Bultmann recognized, the radicality of Jesus' ethical imperatives was *based in his belief that the Kingdom was about to dawn.* Bultmann would not agree with Schweitzer that Jesus proclaimed an "interim ethic,"[38] yet he did agree that "Jesus' demands are in one point to be understood in the light of the eschatological message—namely that in them 'Now' appears as the decisive hour."[39] But existentialism cannot maintain itself as the demythologized form of imminence, for imminence means that *God* is coming, or, as it soon became for Christianity, that the *Parousia* is about to occur. But was not Schweitzer right about the Parousia? Is not the "whole history of Christianity . . . based on the . . . non-occurrence of the parousia"?[40] Can the (existential) imminence of my own future, even if that future is understood as opening the possibility of transcendence to me, really be the modern equivalent of Jesus' belief that God was about to judge the world? For modern man knows that, however imminent his own judgment may always be, the world and its problems will continue.[41] Thus it is precisely the fact that the modern person recognizes himself to be a part of an ongoing world that creates the insurmountable problem for demythologizing at this point, and that forces one to the conclusion that Schweitzer was more correct than Bultmann: Jesus' view of imminence, upon which his ethical preaching was based, was and must remain an eschatological view.

In his *Theology of the New Testament*, Bultmann offered, less extensively, the same interpretation of Jesus' ethical teaching as in *Jesus and the Word*, with the alteration that *agapē* was elevated in importance to be the heading under which radical obedience was discussed.[42] Although Bultmann did not here state that he was seeking "validity" in Jesus' ethical teaching, it is difficult to escape the impression that he was when one reads that love

38. Ibid., pp. 126–29.

39. Ibid., p. 129.

40. Schweitzer, *Quest of the Historical Jesus*, p. 358.

41. In another context, Bultmann explicitly recognizes this fact, but without seeing that it makes a demythologizing of the judgment of the world impossible (Rudolf Bultmann, *The Presence of Eternity* [New York, 1957], p. 153).

42. Bultmann, *Theology of the New Testament*, vol. 1, p. 18.

must be described as an eschatological ethic. For it does not envisage a future to be molded within this world by plans and sketches for the ordering of human life. It only directs man into the Now of his meeting with his neighbor. It is an ethic that, by demanding more than the law that regulates human society does and requiring of the individual the waiver of his own rights, makes the individual immediately responsible to God.[43]

Here, the tension in Bultmann's system between *Jesus and the Word* and his other writings is again no problem, for what Jesus taught about *agapē* then also becomes the mark of Christian existence.[44] Thus one may say that, for Bultmann, Jesus taught more clearly what Christianity also required of Christian existence. But it is still not possible *on these grounds* to grant present validity to the ethical teaching of Jesus, because that teaching becomes unrelated to human existence when the imminence of God's judgment of the world falls away. Bultmann's explanation of the validity of Jesus' ethical teaching thus again encounters the problem that Jesus' eschatological orientation is so related to his ethical imperative that the two cannot be separated, even by demythologizing.

POST-BULTMANNIAN SOLUTIONS

In spite of some aspects of his work that pointed the other way, the over-all impact of Bultmann's work was to focus the attention of a large segment of the New Testament community away from Jesus. By 1953, however, a call was heard from among the Bultmannians to take up the "question of the historical Jesus" again,[45] and the first Bultmannian to answer this challenge was Günther Bornkamm, whose *Jesus of Nazareth* appeared for the first time in German in 1956. Unfortunately, this work represents something of a reversion to a pre-critical stage of New Testament scholarship, so that Bornkamm, especially with regard to the ethical question, accepts most of the Sermon on the Mount as authen-

43. Ibid., p. 19. Here it should be noted that Furnish, *The Love Commandment*, p. 50, has correctly pointed out that the "as yourself" of the love commandment provides a readily understandable criterion for the love of neighbor and does *not* command self love.

44. Bultmann, *Theology of the New Testament*, vol. 1, p. 330.

45. Ernst Käsemann, "The Problem of the Historical Jesus," in *Essays on New Testament Themes*, trans. W. J. Montague, SBT, 41 (Naperville, Ill., 1964), pp. 15–47; the lecture was first delivered in October of 1953 at the Gathering of Former Marburgers.

tically spoken by Jesus and apparently accepts the basic original unity of the passage. To be sure, he acknowledges that chapters 5–7 were "put together by Matthew," but the Sermon on the Mount is nevertheless *the* passage which contains "Jesus' proclamation of the divine will."[46] Quite surprisingly, even, Bornkamm takes two statements in Matt. 5 which almost certainly stem originally from the community lying behind the Gospel of Matthew, or from Matthew himself, to be the key notes of the whole passage. These are Matt. 5:17 ("Think not that I have come to abolish the law and the prophets: I have not come to abolish them but to fulfill them") and Matt. 5:20 ("Unless your righteousness exceeds that of the scribes and Pharisees, you will never enter the Kingdom of Heaven").[47] Bultmann had noted that Matt. 5:17–19 stems from "the discussions between the more conservative (Palestinian) communities and those that were free from the law (Hellenistic)," and that verse 20 "is most probably a heading or introduction by Matthew to 5:21–48."[48] Once this is stated, it is difficult to see how these two verses could be interpreted otherwise.[49]

Accepting this Matthean call to "righteousness" as being from Jesus, Bornkamm sees in the Sermon on the Mount the same existential aspect that Bultmann saw in the "radical demand" of God enunciated by Jesus, i.e., that "the claims of Jesus carry in themselves 'the last things', without having to borrow validity and urgency from the blaze of the fire in apocalyptic scenes. They themselves lead to the boundaries of the world, but do not paint a picture of its end."[50] Bornkamm thus drops the apocalypticism entirely from Jesus' ethical teaching, thereby presumably avoiding the problem of making Jesus' ethics valid for another day;

46. Günther Bornkamm, *Jesus of Nazareth*, p. 100.
47. Ibid.
48. Rudolf Bultmann, *The History of the Synoptic Tradition*, p. 138.
49. Cf. further Georg Strecker, *Der Weg der Gerechtigkeit*, pp. 144 and 151 f. and Ernst Fuchs, *Zur Frage nach dem historischen Jesus*, pp. 100–25, particularly p. 100. Bornkamm elsewhere made it plain, at about the same time, that he agreed with Bultmann's statement on the origin of Matt. 5:17–19; cf. page 24 of his article entitled "End-Expectation and Church in Matthew," in Bornkamm, Barth, and Held, *Tradition and Interpretation in Matthew*. This article first appeared in German in W. D. Davies and D. Daube, eds., *The Background of the New Testament and Its Eschatology: In Honour of Charles Harold Dodd* (Cambridge, 1956), pp. 222–69. Bornkamm's discussion of Matt. 5:20 is ambiguous here, however; cf. pp. 16, 17, and part. 25, where he understands the antithesis as representing Jesus' teaching in spite of Matthew.
50. Bornkamm, *Jesus of Nazareth*, p. 109.

yet, precisely in this attempt to show the insignificance of the
apocalypticism and thus the present validity of Jesus' ethical
teaching, eschatology turns out again to be the insurmountable
problem, for Bornkamm recognizes that Jesus' ethics is an impossible ethics! He characterizes it as a lofty ideal "that again and
again . . . has quickened man's conscience"; but this does not
render it invalid, for "just because it leads so often to a hopeless
tension between God's will and man's ability, it also wakens the
hunger and thirst after righteousness which receives Jesus' promise."[51] But where in the Sermon on the Mount itself is any indication that this is what it was intended to do? Is not the higher
righteousness called for in Matt. 5:20 then given content in considerable detail in what follows? And is not the conclusion of the
chapter ("You shall be perfect!" 5:48) the summation of what has
been indicated before?[52] Is there here any indication that this
passage—even taken uncritically, as Bornkamm largely does—reveals
that Jesus expected anything less than total (radical) obedience?

The understanding of Jesus' ethical teaching as laying down an
ideal toward which one should strive but which is unattainable
prior to the eschaton is of course almost as old as Christianity
itself. Yet such a view can arise only when the eschaton is de-
layed. This can be seen particularly in regard to the command to
love one's enemies.[53] The original form of the command to love
one's enemies, which is surely more nearly to be found in Luke
6:27 than in Matt. 5:44,[54] has nothing in it of the ideal that can
only be approximated. Rather, as the following verses offering for
contrast alternate modes of behavior show, it is absolutely expected that the hearer *is* to love his enemies.[54a] How then can the

---

51. Ibid., p. 109.

52. Cf. Ernst Lohmeyer, *Das Evangelium des Matthäus*, ed. Werner Schmauch,
Meyer Kommentar (Göttingen, 1958), p. 7*; Strecker, *Der Weg der Gerechtigkeit*,
p. 141, n. 2.

53. Cf. the analysis of the fate of the command to love one's enemies given by
Walter Bauer in his essay, "Das Gebot der Feindesliebe und die alten Christen," in
Aufsätze und kleine Schriften, ed. Georg Strecker (Tübingen, 1967), pp. 235–52.

54. Cf. Bultmann, *History of the Synoptic Tradition*, p. 79, who notes the double
parallelism found here in Luke. whereas Luke regularly shortens such passages.

54a. Cf. Wendland, *Ethik des Neuen Testaments*, p. 14, who correctly observes that
the command to love one's enemies gives definition to the command to love one's
neighbor.

Sermon on the Mount, even if one considers only those sayings
that are most likely authentic, be interpreted as offering a to-be-
strived-for ideal? Precisely to the contrary, the command to love
one's enemies expects obedience. That is only possible, however,
if the end has drawn near, as we have already seen in the case of
the parable of the good Samaritan. Once the pressure of imminence begins to be released, the command must be relaxed. This
is normally done by understanding it as an ideal,[55] whereas even
Matthew does not create the Sermon on the Mount as an ideal,
but rather as a paradigm for Christian piety (see especially Matt.
5:13–20). Thus those sayings in the Sermon on the Mount authen-
tically from Jesus can be considered an impossible ethics only if
one is to go on living in the world. If the end of the world has
drawn nigh, bringing with it God's righteousness and judgment,
the "impossible" ethics becomes both possible and consistent.

Bornkamm sees the commandment to love as overcoming the
tension involved in the Sermon on the Mount. As in Bultmann's
Theology of the New Testament, so for Bornkamm love (*agapē*)
is primary and central in Jesus' ethical teaching; "all other commandments are included in this first and foremost one."[56] The
commandment to love means "the renunciation of self-love, the
willingness for and the act of surrender. . . . In this way and no
other God's call comes to us, and in this way the love of God and
the love of our neighbor become one."[57] The parable of the good
Samaritan is taken to give clear expression to this commandment.[58]
Thus the commandment to love becomes for Bornkamm Jesus'
"real" demand, whereas the ethics of the Sermon on the Mount
presents a presently unrealizable ideal. "Jesus never calls [man]
to his ideal destiny, but lays hold of him in what he already is
and does."[59] Bornkamm thus seems to hold that love overcomes
the impossible ethics of Jesus. Yet the love commandment itself is
not at all free of serious difficulties.

55. Alternately, one may, with Johannes Leipoldt, *Der soziale Gedanke in der altchristlichen Kirche*, p. 106, suggest that Jesus really didn't mean it, that he was only employing characteristic oriental imagery, and that what he really intended was "to elucidate the source from which the proper intention springs ever anew."
56. Bornkamm, *Jesus of Nazareth*, p. 110.
57. Ibid., p. 111.
58. Ibid., pp. 112 f.
59. Ibid., p. 117.

In a lengthy criticism and evaluation of Bornkamm's book, in which his own views are of course presented,[60] Ernst Fuchs takes issue precisely with the view that "again and again man can only be referred to what he knows already," i.e., that he can no longer "stand back from the request."[61] The command to love one's neighbor as oneself "betrays," argues Fuchs, "precisely *as* demand an *insurmountable* 'last effort' of the individual 'to stand back' from the demand, thus from love."[62] "Love is never fulfilled," continues Fuchs, "as long as it remains demand."[63] Fuchs had in fact argued in an earlier article that the problem of a commandment to love, by its nature unfulfillable, is overcome christologically. Fuchs reminds us there that "Jesus was given for our sins." "Precisely for this reason," he then adds, "the . . . saying of John 3:16 stands as it were written over the New Testament. That means that the sending of Jesus was an act of God's love in word and deed, on to which we may and must hold as long as we are in the situation of struggling with our own will, with our own natural self-love."[64] Thus, *because of* our standing in this way in God's love, we are both commanded and made capable of loving God and neighbor, as in the Pauline imperative in the indicative.[65] This being in God's love, which is the result of Jesus' having come, is thus the fulfillment of the commandment. But if the commandment is fulfilled, then the Christian must ask *"what remains to be done."*[66] The answer to this question involves what Fuchs calls "something like a Christian ethics." And that something is that the Christian must always "make his behavior, in continual struggle with self-love, into a witness of faith for Jesus Christ."[67] It may thus be observed that Fuchs is attempting to give a doctrinal answer to the problem of the commandment to love, and this is further obvious when he concludes that the com-

---

60. Ernst Fuchs, "Glaube und Geschichte im Blick auf die Frage nach dem historischen Jesus," in *Zur Frage nach dem historischen Jesus*, pp. 168–218.

61. Bornkamm, *Jesus of Nazareth*, p. 117.

62. Fuchs, *Zur Frage nach dem historischen Jesus*, p. 204.

63. Ibid., p. 205.

64. Ernst Fuchs, "Was heisst: 'Du sollst deinen Nächsten lieben wie dich selbst'?" in *Zur Frage nach dem historischen Jesus*, p. 12.

65. Ibid., p. 13.

66. Ibid., p. 15.

67. Ibid.

mandment "possesses true validity only for the believers."[68] This would only mean, however, that, *doctrinally stated*, the Christian says that Jesus himself fulfilled the commandment to love on behalf of the believer. If Fuchs now still wishes to derive from this doctrinal position "something like a Christian ethics," that is all very well, but one must be clear, as regards our present problem, that such a "something" is in no way a guide to moral action. Rather, it becomes a mode of proclamation. To be sure, this is still an ethics in the broader sense of the term, precisely in the same way that Paul was proposing an ethics when he called the celebration of the Lord's Supper proclaiming "the Lord's death until he comes" (1 Cor. 11:26 f.); but this is little help to the modern person who would like to derive from Jesus some guidance or direction, however general or fundamental, for his personal or corporate behavior in a world presenting him with ethical problems.

In his criticism of Bornkamm's book, then, Fuchs argues with sharp insight that love can proceed only from love, not from demand—that is, that the problem one encounters in the commandment to love is that one does not believe in the *power* of love. What the commandment to love really intends to elicit is not obedience to itself as demand, but rather belief in the power of love! But that can occur only where there is love. Only *in* love can one realize "that love really masters our life."[69] Here, therefore, Fuchs seems to move away from the statement of his earlier essay (above) that the commandment to love presents "something like a Christian ethics" to the more thoroughly consistent position that this commandment calls Christian existence into being—that is, in fact calls one to recognize, in faith, that *agapē* is the supremely powerful reality.

In the context of the "new quest of the historical Jesus," Fuchs now distinguishes between present and future aspects of *agapē*. The historical Jesus whom one, in faith, encounters in the proclamation of the gospel is of course the *resurrected* Jesus, the Jesus who takes the burden of the commandment on himself, thus the Jesus in whom one has hope that love will conquer; this is the

68. Ibid., p. 16.
69. Ibid., p. 205.

eschatological aspect of Jesus' preaching. But Jesus also risks everything to his disciples—that is, on them depends the validity of the claim that the Kingdom of God is breaking in at the present in the ministry of Jesus; thus, this Jesus, the *crucified* one, commands his disciples to love because he counts on their loving.[70] Thus Fuchs still does consider the command to love to be valid and to be the command of Jesus; but, even though he uses the term "ethical" as the antithesis to "eschatological,"[71] it would seem that he is no longer speaking even of "something like a Christian ethics" but is rather—by speaking of Jesus' counting on his disciples to love—bringing the Pauline (eschatologically oriented) "imperative in the indicative" into a more general discussion of the place of present and future in Christian existence, and that he is doing this in terms of the historical Jesus—i.e., the Jesus encountered by hearers of the gospel as giving and commanding love. In other words, the historical Jesus, by giving the love commandment, designates Christian existence, which is both imputed and entrusted to the believer in the present in prospect of what is yet to be. If this understanding of *agapē*, however, succeeds in rendering invalid Bornkamm's direct relationship between the commandment and what is expected of the believer, it still cannot be seen to have offered assistance in the formation of a valid and consistent ethics for today, since the orientation toward a future of fulfillment cannot be given up. It goes almost without saying that any attempt to build an ethics on such an understanding of Jesus would have to have as its goal a strictly Christian ethics (by Fuchs' affirmation), one which would realize at the outset that it was unrelated to non-Christians. Perhaps such an ethics would have provided no problem to "Christendom"; but "Christendom" is now a thing of the past, and one would probably have to say that an ethics requiring solid commitment to *one* religion has become unusable in modern American society. It will have to be added that it would be difficult to envisage any way in which love understood as the proclamation involved in the

70. Ibid., p. 211. On p. 214 Fuchs rightly accuses Bornkamm of "falling back into positivism" by trying to handle the commandment to love only from the point of view of Jesus' earthly ministry.

71. Ibid., p. 207.

living of the crucifixion side of the gospel could be related to corporate behavior.

James M. Robinson's book, *A New Quest of the Historical Jesus*, summarizes the whole problem of the historical Jesus, the recent debate, and suggests directions for the further discussion. The point Robinson emphasizes is what he calls "A New Concept of History and the Self." Because "historicism" and "psychologism" are no longer the central concerns respectively of historiography and biography, "the kind of history and biography attempted unsuccessfully for Jesus by the nineteenth century is now seen to be based upon a false understanding of the nature of history and the self." He explains this statement at greater length: "Nineteenth-century historiography and biography were modeled after the natural sciences, e.g., in their effort to establish causal relationships and to classify the particular in terms of the general." This method, however, bypassed "the distinctively historical and human, where transcendence, if at all, is to be found. . . . Today history is increasingly understood as essentially the unique and creative, whose reality would not *be* apart from the event in which it becomes." Thus history should be viewed as "the act of intention, the commitment, the meaning for the participants, behind the external occurrence."[72]

With this definition of history in hand, Robinson believes that a new quest of this *historical* Jesus is possible in which historical would not mean what it meant to all those reviewed in Schweitzer's book, whose historical quest Schweitzer brought to so decisive an end, but rather something like the "historic" Jesus. This historical Jesus would be identifiable with the kerygmatic Christ, since "the *kerygma*," in its decision-invoking function, would presumably continue "Jesus' message; and if the decision called for by Jesus as well as by the *kerygma* was at the basis of his own selfhood, then it is apparent that his person corresponds to its christology."[73] But what does such an approach have to do with ethics?

To be sure, Robinson has not envisioned here practical consequences or a practical application of this theological endeavor, yet the *content* which the new quest of the historical Jesus un-

---

72. James M. Robinson, *A New Quest of the Historical Jesus*, pp. 66 f.
73. Ibid., p. 112.

covers is essentially an ethical content! Robinson defines the unity between Jesus' proclamation and the church's proclamation, hence the new selfhood called for by both Jesus and the *kerygma*, in this way:

> Jesus called upon his hearer to break radically with the present evil aeon, and to rebuild his life in commitment to the inbreaking kingdom. Paul called upon his hearer to die and rise with Christ. Yet when one moves beyond such an initial comparison to the deeper level of meaning, the underlying similarity becomes increasingly clear. To break categorically with the present evil aeon is to cut the ground from under one's feet, to open oneself spiritually to death by renouncing self-seeking as a motivation and giving oneself radically to the needs of one's neighbour, as one's real freedom and love. To do this because of faith in the inbreaking kingdom is to do it in faith that such total death is ultimately meaningful; in it lies transcendence, resurrection. . . . It is this existential meaning latent in Jesus' message which is constitutive of his selfhood, expresses itself in his action, and is finally codified in the Church's *kerygma*.[74]

This understanding of Jesus avoids modernizing Jesus and avoids asking modern man to subscribe to ancient views. It further avoids the problems posed by a belief in God's imminent judgment, and it speaks of transcendence not in the sense of a heteronomous God, which is still the category to which Bultmann's God belongs, but rather in the sense of one's own transcendence. Can this new understanding of Jesus provide a valid ethics for today? Can my acceptance in faith, in response to the Jesus who confronts me in the *kerygma*, of my own death—understood as a death on behalf of others—now be the basis of a consistent and meaningful ethics? To be sure, as in the case of Fuchs, one would have to realize that the ethics implied here is dependent on acceptance of the *kerygma*. It is not related to the non-Christian.

Asking me as a Christian to accept my own death as an existential reality seems in effect to solve the problem of eschatology. If that problem was that I had to anticipate the end of the world, I may now do so existentially, since accepting my death on behalf of others of course entails accepting the death of *my* world and its values. What was significant about the eschatology of Jesus and his followers was that it anticipated the *imminent* end of the

74. Ibid., pp. 122 f.

world. Eschatology is in any case no problem if it only anticipates the *ultimate* end of the world. Astronomy may do the same. But the acceptance of my death means my death *now,* and this must mean also the destruction of my world now. Both these events may be existentially accepted. Yet eventually the ardor with which one embraces such a viewpoint must begin to pale; for my life with its problems goes on, my world and its problems continue. For a few days or weeks, perhaps for a few years, I can accept my own death; but the endurance of the problem-fraught world must finally begin to weigh upon this outlook. Ultimately, I must either give up the death of the world and cling only to my own death—in which case I understand myself to be a derelict—or I must give up the existential stance altogether. It is after all, then, the continual pressure of the *continuous existence of the world and its problems* that finally breaks apart the existentialist attempt to render Jesus' ethics valid. Eschatology has turned out to be a hydra that rears another head even here. In other words, the ethical implications of the new quest of the historical Jesus would appear to be inappropriate to the modern understanding of "world."[75]

Still another possibility to be considered for an ethics that surmounts the problems with which we have been dealing is provided by the Bultmannian who has translated theology into anthropology, Herbert Braun. In his article, "The Problem of a New Testament Theology,"[76] Braun demonstrates that various aspects of New Testament theology involve an understanding of God that is beyond the reach of modern man and that even created problems in the early church before the later books of the New Testament were written. Thus, whereas Jesus viewed the Torah, more specifically its ethical rules, as "entirely binding,"

75. It is the hard alternative posed here that is also overlooked by Richard H. Hiers, *Jesus and Ethics: Four Interpretations* (Philadelphia, 1968), in his otherwise admirable study showing the need to come clean with Jesus' eschatology in any treatment of his ethics. Hiers attempts to demythologize Jesus' eschatology, in the last analysis, by observing that, "as in the case of Jesus' hearers, so for us also, time is short" (p. 165). Knowing that my life is running out, however, is by no means the same as being convinced that the God who vindicates the righteous is just about to come. Just here the difference may be seen, for knowing that I must *finally* die does not lead me to behave in any way as the Samaritan behaves.

76. Herbert Braun, "The Problem of a New Testament Theology," *JThC* 1 (1965): 169–83.

Paul distinguished clearly between law and faith as alternate paths to salvation—the latter, of course, being for him the authentic path.[77] Contemporary with Paul, however, Jewish Christianity emphasized the importance of the Torah, as in Matthew, especially in the Sermon on the Mount; and after Paul the early catholic church no longer saw the distinction he had maintained, as is seen, for example, in the pastoral Epistles.[78] This means that the church could understand theonomy only as heteronomy, could understand God's rule only as expressed in definite commands, frequently subject to casuistic interpretation, and ofttimes simply arbitrary. Jesus, however, in Braun's view, had in reality given the ground rules for overcoming this situation—that is, for Jesus "love toward God is interpreted as love toward one's neighbor."[79] This of course refers to the "Great Commandment," but Braun sees the same principle at work when "the help and kindness demonstrated or not demonstrated to the oppressed neighbor is in fact demonstrated or not demonstrated to Jesus (Matt. 25:31 ff.)."[80] Both Paul and John then take up this same theme.

With Jesus, therefore, we have, according to Braun, *theonomy as autonomy*. Braun refers to the saying about man's being lord of the sabbath and concludes, "Such words of Jesus certainly do not mean that their contents are valid because of Jesus' authority; rather they count on the conscientious Yes of the hearer simply on the basis of their content. In fact, therefore, we have theonomy as autonomy, not as heteronomy."[81] One must not overlook the radicality of this statement for theology. Braun has in effect said that what is valid in the teaching of Jesus has its validity because it is recognized to be valid in and of itself—not because Jesus said it! Thus he can conclude this essay with the following words:

> The word of proclamation and the act of love reach me—if they really do reach me—from my fellow man. God is the whence of my being taken care of and of my being obliged, which comes to me from my fellow man. To abide in God would therefore mean to abide in the concrete act of devoting oneself to the other; whoever abides in *agapan* abides in God (1 Jn. 4:16). I can speak of God

77. Ibid., p. 171.
78. Ibid., pp. 171 f.
79. Ibid., p. 179.
80. Ibid.
81. Ibid., p. 180.

only where I speak of man, and hence anthropologically. . . . That
would mean then, however, that man as man, man in relation with
his fellow man, implies God. That would always have to be discovered anew from the New Testament. God would then be a definite type of relation with one's fellow man. The atheist misses *man*.[82]

One will not be surprised that this same article has then been
reprinted in an anthology as one of several essays dealing with the
phenomenon of the death of God.[83] Thus Braun's Christian ethics,
which seems to be at least ultimately derived from Jesus, would
clearly move beyond the contemporary problem of the loss of
transcendence. If it thus escapes this problem, then of course it
also escapes the problem of the eschatological orientation, since,
as we saw, the problem there lay primarily in the anticipation of
God's imminent judgment. Braun's ethical interpretation of Jesus
is in fact highly commendable in that it lays down no norms, no
middle axioms, hence allows no possibility of casuistry and, although expressed in terms of person-to-person relationships, may
be at least theoretically relevant for the corporate level of ethical
activity (although it must be admitted that the possibility of defining the corporate ethical situation in these terms is uncertain).
It says simply, "I must respond to the need of the other," and it
says no more than that. It is, in a phrase, a totally contextual
ethics.

Braun's ethics presumably remains Christian, it should be
pointed out, in that he states that one is freed to this kind of
ethical responsibility in what he calls the "I may"; but that is, of
course, simply the de-transcendentalized version of forgiveness of
sins. Where Bultmann would have said that one's knowledge of
having received forgiveness freed one to respond to God, and this
response took the form of love of neighbor, Braun prefers to say
that the "I may" and the "I ought" come to me from my fellow
man.[84] Both my being freed and the claim laid upon me come in
the context of interpersonal relationships, and the latter comes
in terms of the former![85] Yet such an understanding of the valid-

82. Ibid., p. 183.
83. Thomas J. J. Altizer, ed., *Toward a New Christianity: Readings in the Death of
God Theology* (New York, 1967), pp. 201–15.
84. Braun, "New Testament Theology," p. 183.
85. Functionally equivalent to Braun's "I may" is Funk's characterization of the
demand to love that is implied in the parable of the good Samaritan as "more a
boon than a demand" (Funk, *Language, Hermeneutic, and Word of God*, p. 216).

ity of Jesus for ethics is not exclusively Christian since, because of the autonomy of the ethical demand, it lays its claim on one not in the context of Christian proclamation, but rather in the human situation itself.

Has this approach thus succeeded in bringing Jesus' ethics into the modern world? Perhaps it has in a sense; but our question in the beginning was whether *Jesus* possessed a validity for ethics today, and this is not what Braun has demonstrated. Rather, by emphasizing that theonomy appeared in Jesus' proclamation as *autonomy* and not as *heteronomy*, he has suggested that any ethical principle coming from Jesus will stand on its own. It does not need Jesus, which means that it possesses its own authority. To turn to Jesus for ethical guidance would be to ask for the imposition of a heteronomy; and Braun makes it clear that the ethical situation is not one in which one asks what Jesus said, or what he did, or even to what existence he calls. One asks rather what one's fellow man needs. And one does not ask this question because one has learned from Jesus that one *should* ask it, rather one asks it simply because the human situation frees one to ask it. That is all. Thus where the best attempt is made to present Jesus as offering an ethics valid for the modern world, Jesus himself is ultimately not important.

One will, of course, have to say that Braun has learned this ethics from Jesus, i.e., from the Great Commandment, the parable of the last judgment, and probably the parable of the good Samaritan. The only question is whether he has thereby done violence to Jesus' teaching. For Jesus, as we have seen, the imminence of God's kingdom made righteousness a pressing matter. This seems to have been because he understood the proclamation of God's nearness to mean not only that one was now freed from self-seeking (Braun's "I may") but that one must also accept the righteousness of the (future) kingdom as already determinative for existence now (Braun's "I ought"). For Braun, however, both freedom and responsibility arise from the ethical situation itself, i.e., autonomously. In the case of the "I ought," one can probably draw a straight line from the parable of the good Samaritan to this point. But the "I may"? Is freedom for selfless ethical behavior the equivalent of the freedom from self-seeking provided by God's imminence? Does not the "I may" arise for Jesus out of the conviction that my destiny—and that of my world—is now for all practical purposes in God's hands? This, as we have seen, is involved in the parable of the good Samaritan, and the same orientation would seem to be the implication of at least the parable of the Pharisee and publican and the parable of the laborers in the vineyard (Matt. 20:1–16)—and certainly of the parable of the last judgment.

In his more recent semi-popular book, *Jesus. Der Mann aus Nazareth und seine Zeit* (Jesus, the Man from Nazareth), Braun has again maintained this same position. He poses the question whether God is not "an entity in and of himself,"[86] and he replies again by emphasizing that Jesus explained love of God as love of neighbor. A few years ago, I had occasion to ask Braun, in conversation, whether, because of these views, he would be willing to describe himself as a humanist who had learned something essential from Jesus. He replied that he would be happy to be so defined. He has obviously, however, also had the term "humanism" put to him as criticism by some who say that he has made of Jesus "only a humanist," and in his Jesus book he meets such criticism. "One has only . . . to replace the word 'humanism' by the New Testament term 'love of neighbor,' and it would then be worth asking whether the 'only' before the term 'love of neighbor' would not come with some difficulty from the mouth of the one who puts forward this objection, insofar as he confronts the Jesus tradition."[87]

Braun seems here, however, to have missed the point. The question is not whether the term "humanism" is used in a pejorative sense ("only" humanism), the negative coloration of which is overcome by the noble New Testament term, "love of neighbor." The question is whether an essential ingredient of Jesus' proclamation has not dropped out in Herbert Braun's explanation, the dropping of which allows one to observe that he has defined Jesus' ethics humanistically, however nobly ("love of neighbor" and not "only humanism").

In this latter work Braun has seen and defined clearly that fundamental ingredient of Jesus' preaching which he labels "Der

86. Herbert Braun, *Jesus. Der Mann aus Nazareth und seine Zeit*, p. 162.
87. Ibid., p. 165.

Horizont der letzten Dinge" (The Horizon of the Last Things).[88]
Like Norman Perrin, he sees that Jesus' emphasis lay less on *what*
was *about* to happen than on "an unprecedented sharpening of
responsibility."[89] "Jesus does not wish to *teach* about the near
end, he wishes to *summon* in view of the near end."[90] Nevertheless, "As unclear as the course of the last things may be in the
proclamation of Jesus, the view, the orientation which underlies
this entire area of proclamation is beyond doubt"; it is the expectation of the imminent coming of the Kingdom of God.[91] It is
then rather confusing how Braun can go from this correct analysis
to the proposal that "essential parts of [Jesus'] proclamation re-
tain their validity, even if the apocalyptic horizon sinks."[92] This
enduring relevance is found, as in the earlier article, primarily in
the love commandment, which does not need an authoritative
Jesus to give it. "Love of neighbor is indeed the center of the
conduct commanded by Jesus."[93] But how can this be? Does
Braun not see the obvious implication of his correct analysis that
the love commanded is unlimited,[94] i.e., that unlimited love is a
possibility for one only if the imminent coming of the Kingdom
of God be presupposed? If we are correct in attributing the freedom involved in the ethical demand stemming from Jesus to his
awareness of the imminence of the righteous God, then we shall
have to say that the removal of the eschatological orientation from
Jesus' ethical teaching would leave a truncated obligation, but
not the organic unity of freedom and obligation Braun finds in
the ethical situation. For Jesus, eschatology is constitutive for
ethics. To disengage the one is to remove the ground for the
other. The ethics proposed by Herbert Braun has much to com-
mend it, but it is not Jesus' ethics, not even Jesus' ethics demythologized.

88. Ibid., pp. 53–61.

89. Ibid., p. 59. Cf. the discussion of Perrin above, p. 4, n. 11. Perrin has over-
stated the case for immediacy; Jesus was interested in immediate responsibility
because of what was about to happen.

90. Braun, *Jesus*, p. 61.

91. Ibid., p. 58.

92. Ibid., p. 61.

93. Ibid., p. 132.

94. Ibid., p. 124: "boundless and measureless."

To put the matter now most sharply, Jesus does not provide a valid ethics for today.[95] His ethical teaching is interwoven with his imminent eschatology to such a degree that every attempt to separate the two and to draw out only the ethical thread invariably and inevitably draws out also strands of the eschatology, so that both yarns only lie in a heap. Better to leave the tapestry intact, to let Jesus, as Albert Schweitzer appealed to us to do, return to his own time. As Cadbury warned, we should avoid the peril of modernizing him. We should let him be a Jew of Palestine of nearly two thousand years ago; let him have his eschatological hopes that were crushed, as Schweitzer said, on the wheel of fate that was his cross; let him believe in the imminent end of the world and God's imminent judgment and, in prospect of that, call his hearers to a radical surrender to God. Only in so doing can we hope to discover the true "historical Jesus." We may even learn to appreciate him more.

95. An ingenious attempt to get around this obstacle has been presented by Ernst Lerle, "Realisierbare Forderungen der Bergpredigt?" *Kerygma und Dogma* 16 (1970): 32–40. Frankly and bluntly stating (p. 37) that the norms of the Sermon on the Mount "are not fully realized in the reality of the people of God," Lerle decides that these can be called simply a "maximal demand" that does not have to be obeyed—because it cannot be obeyed—and that one should look for a "minimal program" (p. 38) which the people of God *are* capable of fulfilling. This "minimal program," then, he finds (pp. 38 f.) in what he calls the principle of "inequality," which he derives from Matt. 7:2b (about being judged with the same judgment as one exercises). Lerle interprets this to mean that one should not expect of others what one does not expect of oneself. Fascinating!

II

THE SYNOPTIC GOSPELS

AND ACTS

In the preceding chapter we were concerned to find any way in which Jesus may be determinative for responsible ethical behavior in the world today, and we reached the conclusion that neither his teaching, nor his life, nor the Jesus who confronts the hearer of the church's *kerygma* is able to transcend the time-bound character of imminent eschatology. Of course, all the noble ethical standards related to Jesus—radical obedience to God's demand, *agapē*, self-giving existence as truly triumphant—are really minor when compared to the most characteristic act to which Jesus called his hearers: repentance.[1] That the primary response to Jesus was expected to be repentance is made clear by Mark 1:15. Since, however, this is a purely religious ethical act, i.e., is in and of itself an act involving only oneself and God and neutral regarding other human beings and the world, repentance has been left out of account in the preceding chapter. It is also to be left out of account here, for the synoptic Gospels agree in placing the same call to repentance in a key position (Mark 1:15 par.). The question now is, then, What ethics do the synoptic Gospels—which, more than any other section of the New Testament, deal explicitly with the earthly Jesus—propose for the Christian's relation to fellow man and world?

MARK AND LUKE (AND ACTS)

Mark, the first canonical writing known as a "gospel," of course passes on the Great Commandment (Mark 12:28 ff.). Since, how-

1. This has been precisely seen by Norman Perrin, *Rediscovering the Teaching of Jesus*, pp. 109–53, who does not even discuss Jesus' ethics as a separate category.

ever, this is placed between Jesus' reply to the question put to him about the resurrection (Mark 12:18–27) and his correcting of the tradition about the Messiah's being David's son (Mark 12:35–37a), it is fairly clear that Mark has intended to show in 12:28–34 not what Christian ethics should be, but rather how Jesus was a better interpreter of Scripture than his contemporaries.[2] In any case, Mark does not otherwise show that he considers this commandment to be an important ethical norm.[3]

Primarily, the Markan ethics is one of discipleship. In the central, climactic section of Mark (8:27–9:10—Peter's confession, first announcement of the passion, saying about coming "after me," and transfiguration) it is clear what the reader (hearer) is to do— he is to "deny himself and take up his cross and follow" Jesus (Mark 8:34; cf. also 8:35–9:1).[4] That "following Jesus" is what Mark had in mind above all when he thinks about what one should do in the world in view of Jesus' having come is made doubly certain by the opening of the public ministry. Immediately after Jesus issues the general call to repentance, he calls the first disciples to "follow after" him (1:17). One must not be misled into thinking that discipleship is limited to a small number, like twelve, because of the tradition of the twelve disciples. (See Mark 3:16–19; note that here Mark apparently deliberately avoids the word "disciple," v. 14.) To the contrary, 8:34 says, "If *anyone* wishes to come after me," and is expressly addressed to "the crowd with his disciples."[5] There can be little doubt as to what content Mark intends to give to "following Jesus"; following Jesus means to suffer with him. Mark 8:34 emphasizes that one must "deny" oneself and "take up" one's "cross."[6]

2. Similarly also Victor Paul Furnish, *The Love Command in the New Testament*, pp. 25–30.
3. Also ibid., p. 74.
4. Regarding v. 34, V. Taylor, *The Gospel According to St. Mark* (London, 1963), p. 381, notes, "In 8.34 three conditions are laid down which must be fulfilled by a loyal follower of Jesus. Two are decisive acts and the third is a continuous relationship." For Mark, this distinction between "act" and "relationship" will hardly hold up, however, since self-denial and the burden of the "cross" also continue. Cf. further below.
5. So also Ernst Lohmeyer, *Das Evangelium des Markus*, p. 171; and Eduard Schweizer, *The Good News According To Mark*, p. 175.
6. Also correctly seen by Ernest Best, "Discipleship in Mark: Mark 8.22–10.52," *ScotJourTheol* 23 (1970): 327–31. Best also gives the necessary distinction that the disciples who follow Jesus do not thereby become little Jesuses! Only Jesus, after all, "gives his life as a ransom for many" (ibid., p. 335; cf. also p. 337).

Left alone, this understanding possesses the possibility of providing a noble, albeit individualistic, ethics. But Mark's discipleship cannot be left with self-denial and taking up one's cross; for one must ask where Jesus is going, i.e., where one is to follow. It is here that the instructions to "watch" and "wait" in Mark 13 take on significance; for Jesus is going not only to the cross, but also to heaven in order to come again (cf. Mark 14:25!), and the suffering that one gets into as a result of following Jesus turns out to be specifically the persecution of the church that is awaiting his Parousia. Thus chapter 13, which begins with Jesus foretelling the persecutions of the church (vv. 9–13), ends with the instruction to "watch, be awake, for you do not know when the time is" (v. 33); and, so that readers of Mark's Gospel will understand that they are included in that injunction,[7] 13:37 summarizes: "What I say to you, I say to all, watch."[8] Thus "the apocalyptic paraenesis takes in a much larger space than the apocalyptic prophecy."[9]

One will have to say, then, that Mark has very little interest in the welfare of the world or its inhabitants other than to persuade as many of them as possible to repent and follow. His imminent eschatology is so much the basis of his outlook that he cannot even pass on Jesus' command to love in its original meaning; instead, he appeals for what one today would have to call retreat from the world and its problems. The Christian's relation to the non-Christian is the endurance of persecution. Regarding how the Christian was expected to relate to his fellow Christian, Mark has almost nothing to say; presumably he conceived of that as no problem, since Christians for the most part simply drew together against the world[10] and in anticipation of the Lord's coming.[11]

7. Lohmeyer, *Evang. des Markus*, p. 286, says of "God's eschatological congregation," "It is there, and its only task is 'to wait and watch.'"
8. The end of the Gospel is, of course, in doubt; but if 16:8 is, as some think, the original ending, then one would be able to say that the note of expectancy on which the Gospel closes is also indicative of Mark's interest in waiting for the Lord to return.
9. Lohmeyer, *Evang. des Markus*, p. 286; similarly also Schweizer, *The Good News*, p. 283.
10. Lohmeyer, *Evang. des Markus*, p. 286, speaks of an "antithesis to the world."
11. James M. Robinson, *The Problem of History in Mark* (Naperville, Ill., 1957), especially lays emphasis on the role of the "eschatological society" in Mark. He notes the significance of the table fellowship as an example of *mores* (pp. 82 f.) and that "some of the instances where Christian custom varies from Jewish custom are of ethical significance" (p. 84), as, e.g., in the saying about divorce (Mark 10:2–12).

If Mark's ethics is determined by his view that the Christian is
a defenseless person awaiting his Lord in a hostile world, that
same ethics is then also endorsed by Luke, who elevates the period
of waiting into a consistent theology.[12] Between Mark and Luke,
however, there is a certain shift of emphasis within this scheme, a
certain replacing of the nuances. Whereas Mark's following Jesus
was enhanced by expectancy, so that "watch" became the watch-
word for Christian ethics, Luke has reckoned explicitly with the
delay of the Parousia and so emphasizes the need for patience or
endurance. As Conzelmann has demonstrated, the verb *hypomenō*,
to endure,[13] although occurring in Luke hardly more frequently
than in Mark, nevertheless may be taken as the most appropriate
term with which to categorize the way in which Luke designates
the Christian's way of being in the world, i.e., his ethics.[14] Thus,
Luke adds "while enduring" onto the end of the interpretation of
the parable of the sower (Luke 8:15), and the Lukan equivalent
to Mark 13:33 (Luke 21:36) enjoins to "be awake *at all times.*"
In Luke 12:35–38, further, Jesus cautions those who are to await
him: "Let your loins be girt up and your lamps burning. And
you are like men awaiting their lord . . . [to] open to him.
Blessed are those servants whom the lord will find watching when
he comes." Verse 38 is especially important: "And if he comes in
the second or in the third watch . . . ." The point is clear, this
"watching" may run on for some time. To this pericope Luke ap-

12. That this is the case for Luke was first demonstrated by Hans Conzelmann in
his book, *The Theology of St. Luke*. Since the appearance of this monograph,
(1st German edition, 1953) many writers have affirmed this thesis, with individual
modifications. One may particularly note, because of its fairly extensive exegetical
analysis, the recent work of Jean-Daniel Kaestli, *L'Eschatologie dans l'oeuvre de Luc*
(Geneva, 1969), especially pp. 17–72. I could by no means agree with the view put
forward by E. Earle Ellis, *Eschatology in Luke* (Philadelphia, 1972), pp. 17 f., that
Conzelmann (and Bultmann) have fallen victim to the fallacy of the Hegelian
dialectic (why must it be a fallacy?) by proposing: imminent expectation (thesis),
delay of Parousia (antithesis), Luke's *Heilsgeschichte* (synthesis); whereas, one
should ask, "But where is the evidence that the nonoccurrence of the parousia was
a crucial problem that had to be resolved?" I am of the opinion that Conzelmann
has adequately demonstrated the problem of the delay, and attestation of that
problem in Luke is also found in the paragraphs below.

13. That *hypomenō* more nearly means "endure" than "be patient" has, I think,
been demonstrated by Schuyler Brown, *Apostasy and Perseverance in the Theology
of Luke*, pp. 48–50. This is not really contrary to Conzelmann's thesis, but rather
substantiates the view that Luke thinks of an extended time before the Parousia
during which the Christian must "hold out."

14. Cf. Conzelmann, *Theology of St. Luke*, p. 231.

pends the Q saying about the householder not knowing when in the night the thief may be coming (Luke 12:39 f. par.). Conzelmann seems adequately to have expressed Luke's ethical view at this point:

> The shift of emphasis in eschatology brings about of its own accord a change of structure in ethical thinking. Out of the life within the eschatological community with its expectation of an imminent End, there now emerges the "vita Christiana." The Judgement still remains a motif, no longer on account of its proximity, but because it is a fact.[15]

The same persecutions which evoked Mark's "watch" call forth for Luke the suggestion that the Christian must be patient, must endure. In the Lukan version of the synoptic apocalypse, chapter 21, Luke makes it clear that the church must *pass through* the evil days which are, in the more original form of the apocalypse (Mark 13), the signs that the end is at hand. Of the "wars and rumours of wars" (Mark 13:7) both Mark and Matthew say that "they must occur, but the end is not yet." Luke (21:9) changes to "wars and uprisings" and says of them, "These things must occur *first*, but the end is not *immediately*." At the first of verse 12, Luke adds what is not present in Mark or Matthew, *"Before all these things they will lay their hands upon you and persecute you,"* and then he picks up Mark again. Given the realization gained from recent study of Luke that he expects some time to elapse before the Lord comes, it is clear that he does not take persecution of the church necessarily to presage the end. Conclusive is his alteration of Mark 13:13b ("The one who remains to the end, he will be saved," implying that the Lord will come when the woes come to their end): "By your endurance you *will* gain your lives."

For Luke, of course, as Conzelmann has shown, the present of the church is the present of receiving the message of the Kingdom of God, of being granted forgiveness, and of anticipating the Kingdom.[16] This being the case, it is to be expected that Luke

---

15. Ibid., p. 232. See also William C. Robinson, Jr., *Der Weg des Herrn*, trans. Gisela and Georg Strecker, Theologische Forschung, 36 (Hamburg-Bergstedt, 1964), p. 66.

16. Conzelmann, *Theology of St. Luke*, pp. 207–34, particularly pp. 225–31. Whether this present is also intended by Luke to be designated as Kingdom of God is still, in my opinion, an open question. Conzelmann argues for a strictly future view of the Kingdom in Luke, and is defended by William C. Robinson, Jr., against Philipp Vielhauer, who is of the opposite opinion. But Luke 17:20–32 is not to be understood too easily one way or the other.

will move in the direction of designating more adequately than
Mark the marks of a Christian life this side of the Parousia—that
is, of a Christian ethics which reckons with an ongoing world.
That Luke does this only to a disappointingly slight degree is only
indicative of the built-in problem of trying to deal with one's life
in the world when, by all rights, that world should have passed
away already, and God should have taken over the responsibility
for the quality of one's life. Thus, the best that Luke does is to
designate such bland virtues as "goodness and justice" (Luke
23:50) or "full of the Holy Spirit and faith" (Acts 11:24, where
goodness is also included).[17]

Contrary to a notion that exists in some quarters, Luke does not
suggest or imply any more detailed or explicit guidelines for life
in the world during the extended time of awaiting the Parousia.[18]
Cadbury has dealt with such possibilities[19] and has indicated that
the suggestion that Luke is interested in the use of money offers
the strongest possibility for finding in Luke a specific guideline
for the Christian's relation to the world. Cadbury sees in Luke
the possibility of a concept of Christian stewardship of money—
to be sure, not related to the needs of the underprivileged but
rather to a concept of duty on the part of the financially privi-
leged.[20] Such a view would be related to "Old Testament piety,"
and "its roots lie deep in the social ideals and apocalyptic hopes
which the evangelist inherited."[21] It is true that there are several
references to money in Luke not found in the other Gospels. In
every instance, however, the presence of money in a saying owes
its existence to the fact that some use of money is picked up as an

17. Furnish, *The Love Command*, pp. 84–90, also finds "doing good" to be the
paramount expression of Luke's ethics, although he perhaps goes too far in arguing
for the Lukan view of sharing one's possessions. Cf. further immediately below.

18. Such a position is maintained, for example, by Johannes Leipoldt, *Der soziale
Gedanke in der altchristlichen Kirche*, pp. 140–56. Leipoldt sees this aspect of Luke
as related in part to his missionary interest, i.e., Luke seeks to make Christianity
attractive to certain groups (pp. 152–56).

19. Henry J. Cadbury, *The Making of Luke-Acts*, pp. 258–65. Regarding the supposed interest of Luke in women, Cadbury notes, "His interest may be described
rather as artistic or domestic or sentimental," p. 263.

20. Ibid., pp. 262 f. Cf. further Heinz-Dietrich Wendland, *Ethik des Neuen Testaments*, p. 39, who proposes a still different possibility for Luke's attitude toward
money, i.e., that "Luke accentuates the discarding of riches essentially more sharply
than does Matthew."

21. Ibid., p. 262.

illustration of something else, i.e., "money" occurs in Luke as a commonplace and no more than that. Thus, in the parable of the two debtors (Luke 7:41–43), there is clearly a defense of Jesus' association with unrighteous people—that is, a defense against the charge made in verse 39. The parables of the unjust steward (Luke 16:1–9) and of the rich man and Lazarus (Luke 16:19–31) are utilized by Luke to show how the Pharisees cannot interpret the law aright.[22] That Luke here and elsewhere calls the Pharisees "lovers of money" is probably merely a slander and unrelated to any possible "Christian approach to money." Concerning Luke's understanding of the parable of the pounds (Luke 19:11–27), Jeremias correctly notes that one can see in 19:11 how Luke understood this parable. "Over against a fanatical expectation of the Parousia, Jesus announces the putting off of the Parousia and explains the reason: the time in between is a time of testing for his disciples."[23] If Luke has any particular interest in money, it involves an understanding that money is a part of "this world" and hence is to be forsaken in prospect of the coming Kingdom. The saying in 12:15 and the following parable of the rich fool (Luke 12:16–21) seem, in fact, to say just this, and the same point is more or less involved in the parable of the tower builder (Luke 14:28–30). The "cost" of this last parable, however, clearly provides the same element as the "powerful" of the following parable of the king going to war (v. 31)—that is, a risk is involved. Surely, Luke provides his understanding of these two parables in verse 33: ". . . who does not renounce all his possessions . . . ." We are forced to conclude that Luke's "interest" in money has nothing to do with an understanding of the relation of Christian to fellow man and world. Rather, it shows a rejection of the world characteristic of early Christian eschatology. Luke has not altered the view of world that is ingredient to that eschatology. He has only resigned himself to a longer existence of the world than was first expected.[24]

22. For further evidence that this is the case, cf. my article, "Tradition and Redaction in Luke xv. 11–32," *NTS* 15 (1969): 437 f.

23. Joachim Jeremias, *Die Gleichnisse Jesu* (Göttingen, 1962), pp. 56 f.

24. The qualification of Conzelmann's explanation of Luke's theology suggested by S. G. Wilson, "Lukan Eschatology," *NTS* 15 (1970): 330–47, that Luke "did not expect the Church to continue for 2,000 years" (p. 346) is certainly to be accepted,

What, however, of the parable of the good Samaritan (Luke 10:29–37)? Did not Luke, by including this parable from his special material, give considerable content to what he meant by "goodness"? If this parable was in fact intended by Luke to give a specific color to his ethical concept, then that color is immediately toned down considerably by the following pericope, the narrative of Mary and Martha (Luke 10:38–42), where precisely the one who does care for physical needs is devaluated in favor of the one who sits at the Lord's feet. These two pericopes can hardly be brought into an ethical unity, even if Luke intended them both to be ethical examples.

In spite of the fact, however, that the parable of the good Samaritan does not quite answer the question (Luke 10:29) arising out of the Great Commandment (cf. the conclusion of the parable, v. 36: "Who of these three appears to you to have been a neighbor . . . ?"),[25] it does seem most likely the case that Luke intended the parable to be a commentary on the command to love one's neighbor. Luke thus probably understood the parable to explain that loving one's neighbor meant primarily helping the neighbor if he were in need. It may well be, then, that what Luke meant by his vague "good man" was in fact one who loves his neighbor in the manner demonstrated by the parable of the good Samaritan. Since this theme is not elsewhere taken up by Luke, however, one will have to realize that it plays only a minor role for him.

Aside from what Luke himself thought of the importance of this parable, it would not be illegitimate for the modern Christian to exalt Luke's understanding of it, with the attached command to love, to a place of supreme ethical importance, and to say that Christian ethics should be essentially love of one's neighbor in

---

since it is true that, for Luke, "the end was a sure hope that would be fulfilled in the near future" (p. 346). This will be the proper explanation for those sayings and portions of Luke that belong to what Wilson calls the "imminent expectation strand" (pp. 340–44). That this explanation damages Conzelmann's thesis, however, I would disagree, since, as Wilson also notes, "in Acts there is no imminent expectation" (p. 347). To propose, however, that the delay/imminent expectation strands in Luke and the absence of imminent expectation from Acts rest upon Luke's pastoral concern in a shifting pastoral situation (pp. 344–47) is to reduce Luke's theological interest unnecessarily.

25. Cf. Rudolf Bultmann, *The History of the Synoptic Tradition*, p. 178.

the way demonstrated by the parable of the good Samaritan. Here, the problem of an interim ethics would not arise, since Luke precisely counts on a somewhat expanded period of world history before the Parousia, a period in which the church will await the coming of its Lord, but individuals may not live to see that day. Here would be a truly noble ethical ideal, and one might even say that it would be true to Luke's "spirit," if not to his intent—that is, had Luke survived the centuries since his own day, he might today give a higher place to this example of aiding one's fellow man.

Beloved as this ideal of love of one's fellow man is among Christians today—love understood as helping someone in need—it is not without its difficulties, perhaps overwhelming ones. Aside from those which the study of ethics itself would raise (What *is* good for my fellow man? How can what is good for him be decided? In what way can society function ethically on this principle?), there would remain the considerable problem of retaining the command to love as valid, while removing what Wilder refers to as the "eschatological sanction." How can one live under such a command *continuously*? Jesus expected the Kingdom to come soon, thus obviating any such problem, as was demonstrated in chapter 1; but that was not Luke's view, and we have no indication from Luke that he even saw the problem.

It can be granted that this ethical ideal—love of one's neighbor understood as caring for the needs of one's fellow man—which admittedly plays an unimportant role in Luke's Gospel, is one which many will wish to endorse. It presents so many difficulties, however, that one can hope that something less confusing, more direct, and more practical is forthcoming.

We grant Luke our sympathy. He was in a difficult situation theologically. He wanted to hold on to the orientation toward the future as in Mark (and in the rest of early Christianity generally); hence, he retained the "watching" and "waiting," and he accommodated these motifs to his view of a somewhat extended time before the Parousia by emphasizing the need for endurance and for living through times of persecution. This orientation, however, is ultimately fatal for his ethical perspective; for he is unable seriously to deal with the problem of responsible ethical behavior and offers only a vague glimpse of what one's ethics should be, i.e., one should be good.[26]

Acts adds nothing materially to the view of Christian ethics one finds in the third Gospel. Aside from the "virtues" given above, there is only the realization that "the Christian life is a 'way' and inevitably leads through many tribulations (Acts 14:22)."[27] Conzelmann rightly notes that Acts presents to the church an ideal neither of poverty nor of community of possessions. Especially the latter is "the stylized account of the unity of the Church."[28]

MATTHEW

The author of the first Gospel, one is now able to note, did not make of the problem of the delay of the Parousia, as did Luke, a consistent theology, although he was certainly aware of the problem.[29] (Most often, the parable of the wise and foolish virgins, Matt. 25:1–13, is cited as evidence of this fact.) One might say, however, that, if Matthew was less able than Luke to deal theoretically with the delay, he nevertheless made a much more thorough attempt to deal with the extended interim on a practical level; for he is in large part concerned with Christian life.

"Unless your righteousness exceed that of the scribes and Pharisees," cautions Matthew in a key passage (5:20), "you shall not enter the Kingdom of Heaven." Not only does this serve as an introduction to the remainder of the Sermon on the Mount, but it provides one of the major themes—perhaps *the* major theme —of the Gospel. Immediately prior to this, Matthew had had Jesus say, "Do not think that I came to destroy the law or the prophets; I did not come to destroy but to fulfill" (5:17); and this view of Jesus coincides with the Matthean insertion placed on the lips of Jesus explaining why he (the perfect one) submitted to John's baptism: "to fulfill all righteousness" (3:15).[30] When Matthew then draws to the close of his account of the public ministry with

26. Brown, *Apostasy and Perseverance*, p. 121, observes that "the Lucan emphasis is . . . on philanthropy or 'good works.'"
27. Conzelmann, *Theology of St. Luke*, p. 234.
28. Ibid., p. 233.
29. See particularly Georg Strecker, *Der Weg der Gerechtigkeit*, pp. 41–49.
30. Cf. C. G. Montefiore, *The Synoptic Gospels*, vol. 2 (London, 1927²), ad loc.

Jesus' tirade against the Pharisees for not pursuing the true righteousness which is the law's intent (ch. 23), he thus makes it abundantly obvious that the law is the thing for the first Gospel and that Matthew has represented Jesus as the one who lays down the Christian law. The "everything which I commanded you" of the last verse of the Gospel makes such a conclusion absolutely unavoidable.

Gerhard Barth is of the opinion that Matthew does not present Jesus as the giver of a *new* law, but as the true *interpreter* of the already existent law, i.e., law and prophets (which are not distinguished), and that the ground or insight on the basis of which Jesus does this is the command to love.[31] This view is probably correct. The first section of the body of the Sermon on the Mount (the antitheses, 5:21–47) concludes with the command to love one's enemies, and there immediately follows the summary statement, "You therefore will be perfect" (5:48). Gerhard Barth argues that, because of this concluding statement and because of the position of the saying about loving one's enemies as last in the list of antitheses, the command to love one's enemies is the climax of the antitheses.[32] Obviously, the antitheses are intended as a paradigmatic explanation of 5:20 (righteousness exceeding that of scribes and Pharisees)—that is, Matt. 5:21–47 offers prime examples of how the Christian may know what he must do in order for his righteousness to exceed the normative concept of Jewish righteousness.[33] The passage "does not denote a 'more' in the sense of

31. Gerhard Barth, "Matthew's Understanding of the Law," in *Tradition and Interpretation in Matthew*, by Günther Bornkamm, Gerhard Barth, and Heinz Joachim Held, pp. 75–105. So also Hans Conzelmann, *An Outline of the Theology of the New Testament*, p. 146. M. Jack Suggs, *Wisdom, Christology, and Law in Matthew's Gospel* (Cambridge, Mass., 1970), pp. 109–27, has sought to show that this *interpretative* function of Jesus is a part of Matthew's presentation of Jesus as Wisdom and consequently as "the embodiment of Torah" (p. 127). The Sermon on the Mount does indeed, as Suggs, p. 127, points out, refer to the "wise (*phronimos*) man" who heeds Jesus' words, and Suggs might have referred further to the long wisdom passage, Matt. 6:25–34. Suggs may indeed be correct, although I suspect that the connection is not as obvious as Suggs seems to make it—that is, Matthew more likely thinks of Jesus as out-trumping Wisdom just as he out-trumps Moses. That would be the point of the Q saying in 12:41 f. (overlooked by Suggs) that Jesus is greater than Jonah (the prophet) and Solomon (the sage).

32. Barth, *Tradition and Interpretation*, p. 80; cf. further on this point Furnish, *The Love Command*, pp. 45–54.

33. Also correctly seen by Paul Hoffmann, "Der ungeteilte Dienst. Die Auslegung der Bergpredigt (Mt 6, 1–7, 27)," *Bibel und Leben* 11 (1970): 89–104.

the quantitative or extensive, but the intensive."[34] These antitheses show that the way to know what is Christian righteousness
is to interpret the law aright, and that means to understand it in
an intensified way. The quality of this intensifying is then given
by the command to love—in this case, to love one's enemies.
Chapter 23 also points in this direction.[35]

The way in which the Great Commandment is presented in
Matthew further shows that Matthew intends to intensify the law
on the basis of the command to love. Matthew concludes the command to love God and to love one's neighbor with the summary
statement (not found in Mark or Luke), "In these two commandments, *all the law and the prophets* are caught up" (Matt. 22:40).
Thus we have here, in Gerhard Barth's words, a "concentration of
the whole law on one point, in which everything is contained."[36]
If this now begins to sound slightly reminiscent of Rom. 13:9,
". . . and if there is any other commandment, it is summed up in
the saying, 'You shall love your neighbor as yourself,' " that similarity is far more apparent (linguistic) than real (material); for
what Paul means is that the Torah may be dispensed with in
view of the all-inclusive command to love, whereas Matthew views
the command to love as "principle of interpretation,"[37] on the
basis of which one may reinterpret the Torah. Matthew thus
endorses a *Christian casuistry* in which the command to love
provides in each case the direction in which one moves when
attempting to derive the particular guide for conduct from the
Torah.

This casuistry is, however, by no means the whole of the way
in which Matthew develops his Christian ethics; for he also takes
up in a deliberate way the Christian *lex talionis* that arose probably in the preaching of the early Christian prophets.[38] This kind

34. Barth, *Tradition and Interpretation*, p. 98. Cf. further Martin Dibelius, "Die
Bergpredigt," in *Botschaft und Geschichte*, vol. 1 (Tübingen, 1953), p. 93: The
Sermon on the Mount "sets up a programme of Christian ethics for the church
for all time."
35. Cf. further 24:12 f. and the comments on chap. 24 by Rudolf Pesch, "Eschatologie und Ethik. Auslegung von Mt 24, 1–36," *Bibel und Leben* 11 (1970): 223–38.
36. Barth, "Matthew's Understanding," p. 77.
37. Ibid., p. 85.
38. For this insight I am of course indebted to Ernst Käsemann, "Sentences of Holy
Law in the New Testament," in *New Testament Questions of Today*, pp. 66–81; the
article was first published in 1954. Käsemann has argued convincingly, primarily on

of ethical teaching comes most clearly to expression in Matthew in 6:14 f., "For if you forgive men their transgressions, your heavenly father will also forgive you; but if you do not forgive men, neither will your father forgive your transgressions." Whether this is a more original form of the saying than that found in the parallel, Mark 11:25,[39] or whether Matthew has altered the Markan saying to bring it more exactly into the proper form need not concern us here. Clearly, Matthew has here related an ethical norm to something other than the command to love—the *character of eschatological judgment.* This same way of putting the ethical norm is found in a somewhat impure form even prior to this, in Matt. 5:19: "Whoever relaxes one *of the least* of these commandments and teaches men so *will be called least* in the Kingdom of Heaven." That these tenets of holy law are not disconnected elements in Matthew, unrelated to his over-all ethical view, is attested by several observations. Käsemann calls attention especially to Matt. 16:27,[40] which adds to Mark 8:38b (the Son of man is coming "in the glory of his father with the angels"), "and then he will repay each according to his deed." Further, the eschatological *lex talionis* regarding forgiveness so clearly stated in 6:14 f. also finds expression, in parabolic form, in a widely separated section of Matthew, the parable of the unforgiving servant (Matt. 18:23–35; without parallel in Mark or Luke).[41] Even the very fact that this form of *lex talionis* is found in the introduction to the antitheses of the Sermon on the Mount (Matt. 5:19)—and with emphatic reference to the *whole* law—attests the importance Matthew gives to this way of putting the ethical standard.

---

the basis of Rev. 22:18 f., for the origin of the form of eschatologically oriented apodictic tenets of holy law in early Christian prophecy. This point will not be debated here. That Matthew, far more than the other synoptic Gospels, employs this form of ethical teaching, and attributes it to Jesus, will of course be obvious; cf. further below.

39. The form of a tenet of holy law is defined as close terminological agreement between protasis and apodosis in a pronouncement in which the protasis determines (by a "whoever" or "if you [or one]" or "he who") the future (apocalyptic) divine reaction given in the apodosis. Cf. Käsemann, *New Testament Questions of Today,* p. 67. In this particular instance (Matt. 6:14 f.) Käsemann would apparently hold that the Matthean form is more original (cf. p. 77).

40. Ibid., p. 77.

41. Barth, *Tradition and Interpretation,* p. 84, views this parable as a further example of the influence of the command to love on Torah exegesis. In this, he appears to have overlooked the connection with Matt. 6:14 f.

The situation seems to be that Matthew, on the one hand, views the law (as interpreted by the Great Commandment) as both way of salvation and standard for Christian existence; and, on the other hand, he accepts in an unqualified way the validity of the apocalyptic *lex talionis*, expressed in the form of arbitrary divine tenets, for determining what Christian existence should be. That he views the law both as way of salvation and as ethical norm falls in with the observation that Matthew distinguishes at least equally as sharply between Christians who are going to obtain righteousness—and the Kingdom of Heaven—and those who are not, as between Christians and non-Christians. Thus he can assert that "many are called but few chosen" (Matt. 22:14), and he can argue sharply against "false prophets" (7:15–20), saying of them that "not everyone who says to me, 'Lord, Lord!' will enter the Kingdom of Heaven, but the one who does the will of my father in heaven" (7:21). This seems to mean that the prophets, who merely prophesy, cast out demons in the Lord's name, and do many miraculous deeds, also in his name (7:22; the point must not be overlooked that they thereby give every indication of being under the power and guidance of the Spirit) will not enter the Kingdom of Heaven; whereas, the one who builds his life on the foundation of the preceding teaching in 5:3 ff. will (7:24–27).

The consistent mentioning of entering the Kingdom of Heaven in the preceding paragraph is not amiss and is precisely in the meaning of Matthew. (The phrase "to enter the Kingdom of Heaven" alone occurs five times in Matthew, not to mention such phrases as "precede you into the Kingdom of Heaven," "yours" or "theirs is the Kingdom," and "least" or "greatest in the Kingdom of Heaven.") It seems to be Matthew's preoccupation with entering the Kingdom that allows him to mingle the apocalyptic *lex talionis* together with the Torah as interpreted by the Great Commandment. Both point to the Lord's coming! Both would fall out if the Lord really were not coming.[42] The "true" Christian is for Matthew the one who strives for righteousness that he

---

42. Georg Strecker, "Die Makarismen der Bergpredigt," *NTS* 17 (1971): 255–75, has also made it clear that such is the orientation precisely for the programmatic introduction to the Sermon on the Mount, the Beatitudes. In each Beatitude, the first clause is "uniformly ethically accented," whereas the second clause is "uniformly . . . related to the eschatological future" (p. 271).

may enter the Kingdom;[43] way of salvation and character of Christian existence are thus one and the same.

In spite of Matthew's eschatological orientation, one might wish, as in the case of Luke, to excerpt his principle of interpreting law by the standard of love for neighbor from its intended context. (There would then be no need to stay with the *Jewish* law.) But immediately the impossibility of this would become obvious for, as was noted above, that interpretation leads Matthew to an *intensification*—not murder but *anger*, not adultery but *lust*. This is the *way* in which Matthew wished to interpret law by love. But what organized society would begin to operate on such principles? Even viewed as limited to individual ethics, this principle would have to perish under the insights of psychology that man does not live without "lusts of the flesh." In spite of the fact that Matthew has, by his ethical organization of the tradition of Jesus' teaching, dealt seriously with the delay of the Parousia, what he proposes is nevertheless so bound up with the expectation of that Parousia that it would be preposterous in the time of the non-occurrence of the Parousia.

As was the case with Mark and Luke, Matthew endorses such virtues as humility, not giving offense, and "rescuing the perishing" (Matt. 18:1–14). All such instances of "congregational ethics," however, fall under the heading of Matthew's Christian piety, which he himself labels being "poor in spirit" (5:3). But Matthew makes it clear: "Blessed are the poor in spirit, *for theirs is the Kingdom of Heaven*," i.e., the various pious virtues (more or less detailed in the Beatitudes, 5:3–11) are the specifics of the ethical understanding involved in the eschatological *lex talionis*. If I behave thus and so now, God will reward me in the Kingdom.[44] Matt. 6:1–18 gives a particular place of esteem to almsgiving, praying, and fasting; but these congregational virtues have heavenly reward especially in view, as the thrice repeated "the Father . . . *will give* you" shows. As if this alone were not emphatic

---

43. Cf. Hans Windisch, *The Meaning of the Sermon on the Mount*, trans. S. MacLean Gilmour (Philadelphia, 1951), p. 27; Günther Bornkamm, "End-Expectation and Church in Matthew," in *Tradition and Interpretation in Matthew*, p. 16.

44. Strecker, *Weg der Gerechtigkeit*, p. 223, calls such a passage as 18:1–14 merely "normal demands of congregational ethics." There is more than that involved in these little pious virtues for Matthew—the gaining of the Kingdom.

enough, Matthew caps off this section with the saying about storing up treasures in heaven (6:19–21).

Matthew is also a strong proponent of discipleship.[45] He seems not to distinguish disciples, however, as a special group within Christianity; hence, nothing new is provided here for his ethical understanding.

We may let George Strecker have the last word regarding Matthew's ethics:

> Finally, it is clear that Christian existence is essentially stamped by the salvation-history understanding of the congregation. On its course through time, the congregation aligns itself with the holy past and at the same time lives with a view toward the future for which the reward—as the final foundation and conclusion of its eschatological being that is realized ever anew in discipleship—is promised to it. In this way the relation of the individual to the eschatological imperative is also temporally determined.[46]

45. See a concordance for *akoloutheō*, *deute*, and *mathēteuō*.
46. Strecker, *Weg der Gerechtigkeit*, p. 235.

III

PAUL

Paul's ethical admonitions are linked to those of Matthew in a surprising way; next to Matthew, Paul makes the most use of tenets of holy law.[1] In 1 Cor. 3:17, Paul warns, "If anyone spoils the temple of God, God will spoil him," and in 1 Cor. 14:38, "If anyone does not know, he is not known." Not quite in the proper form, but clearly revealing the orientation in eschatological judgment to which Käsemann has called attention, is 1 Cor. 16:22, "If anyone does not love the Lord, let him be anathema." To this, Paul adds immediately, "*Marana tha* [our Lord, come],"[2] thereby showing that the threat of anathema lies in the judgment at the Parousia rather than in the authority of the church or of the apostle. A formulation similar to that of 1 Cor. 16:22 occurs in Gal. 1:9, "If anyone proclaims to you a gospel different from what you received, let him be anathema."[3] The business in 1 Cor. 5:3–5 about Paul's excommunicating the chap who has been immoral is also precisely tied in with this aspect of Paul's ethics,[4] as the concluding statement there shows: the offender is to be turned over to Satan "in order that his spirit may be saved in the day of the Lord."[5]

1. Cf. Ernst Käsemann, "Sentences of Holy Law in the New Testament," in *New Testament Questions of Today*, pp. 66–81. It is unfortunate that the recent work of Heinz-Dietrich Wendland, *Ethik des Neuen Testaments*, overlooks entirely the existence of tenets of holy law.

2. Cf. the discussion of the proper translation of this Aramaic acclamation by Hans Conzelmann in *Der erste Brief an die Korinther* (pp. 360 f.), an English translation of which is soon to be published by Fortress Press in the Hermeneia series.

3. Cf. further 2 Cor. 9:6 and Rom. 2:12. Closely related to this motif is in fact the whole passage, Rom. 1:18–2:3.

4. Cf. Käsemann, *New Testament Questions of Today*, pp. 70–72.

5. In addition to revealing the eschatological orientation of the judgment, this statement of course also shows that Paul considers the *purpose* of pronouncing the judgment of the eschaton to be salvific; cf. Käsemann, ibid.

While Paul's use of tenets of holy law ties him in a certain way
to the same tradition found in Matthew, there is at the same time
a distinct difference in the *way* Paul uses these eschatological pronouncements. Matthew employs them to urge Christians to "store
up treasures in heaven," i.e., to build up a supply of righteousness
done, such as forgiveness, so that they may enter the Kingdom.
Paul, on the other hand, never mentions such a theme. (The
closest he comes to doing so is Gal. 5:19–21, where he explains
what sorts of things a Christian may *not* do and still "inherit the
Kingdom of God.") Paul rather uses the tenets of holy law absolutely—that is, they are unrelated to any general goal or to any
general ethical norm. These pronouncements are divinely derived
and bear their own immediate authority.[5a] Clearly, they are related
to an immediate, particular situation; in view of the situations in
Corinth and Galatia that called forth the letters respectively of
1 Corinthians and Galatians, one might even say that Paul employed tenets of holy law in critical or crisis situations. Yet the
methodical and even cool way in which he explains in Rom. 1:18–
2:3 that certain actions by gentiles lead inevitably to certain related
manifestations of divine wrath would lead one to conclude that
Paul assigned a larger role to arbitrary, reciprocal eschatological
judgment than might be inferred from the four occurrences of
tenets of holy law in 1 Corinthians and Galatians.

Here is then one aspect of Paul's ethics that rejects the imposition of any system. His use of tenets of holy law reveals a side of
his ethics that is arbitrary, absolute, and altogether to be explained
from his belief in imminent eschatological divine judgment. It
may be that Paul uses these divine pronouncements more or less
in the sense of what may be aptly called the imperative in the
indicative,[6] i.e., to help prevent Christians from giving up their

---

5a. This is more or less dimly seen by Wendland, *Ethik des Neuen Testaments*,
p. 86, who tries to express Paul's ethics in terms of the alternatives, "norm ethics"
and "situation ethics," and who concludes that "it is a matter of norms for concrete
situations."

6. This relationship of imperative to indicative seems first to have been seen by
Rudolf Bultmann, "Das Problem der Ethik bei Paulus," *ZNW* 23 (1924): 126, who
put the relationship of indicative to imperative as "grounding the imperative on
the *fact* of justification, *drawing* the imperative *from* the indicative," and who
pointed to Gal. 5:25, "If we live by the Spirit, let us also follow the Spirit." Victor
Paul Furnish, *Theology and Ethics in Paul*, p. 225, argues against Bultmann that
"the Pauline imperative is not just the result of the indicative but fully integral to
it." This is Bultmann's meaning, however. Bultmann did not mean "result" by
"grounding" and "drawing from," but explained rather that "the *dikaiōtheis* is the

justified, "rightwised," position.[7] Nevertheless, the imperative of the tenets of holy law is not *based upon, grounded in* the indicative of justification as is otherwise normally the case for the ethical imperatives Paul uses. Rather, the grounding for the tenets of holy law is plainly and simply the eschatological judgment. If that falls out, so do the imperatives based upon it.

In Paul's use of these pronouncements of divine, eschatologically oriented law, one of course sees an earlier stage of their use than in Matthew. For Paul, the divine pronouncement of judgment stands on its own as given by God; for Matthew, it has the function of forming a part of the paradigm for righteousness which one must fulfill if one is to enter the Kingdom. In this case, therefore, whereas for Paul the Christian stands always before the awesome judgment of a righteous God, for Matthew the righteousness is a paradigm for living, a way of salvation. Stated in other terms, God's (new) law is for Matthew a given; for Paul, however, one awaits its being given. For Matthew, divine law impinges upon the present from the past—for Paul, from the future.[6a] This difference between Paul and Matthew may well be viewed as a necessary and inevitable concomitant of the delay of the Parousia. As time elapsed, after Paul's day, it surely became increasingly difficult for the church to recognize the authority claimed for such arbitrary judgments. The safe thing to do was to grant authority only to those tenets of holy law given in the past, i.e., by an apostle or, better, by the Lord himself when he was on earth. Once *new* pronouncements had to take second place to *old*, once the tension of standing always before the judge was relaxed, Matthew's use of divine law was a natural next step. But the problems of maintaining the language of imminent eschatology after the eschatology has ceased to be imminent only lead, as was seen in the preceding chapter, into an impossible ethical situation.

When Paul cites a saying of the Lord—something that occurs

concrete man who bears the burden of his past, present, and future, who also stands, therefore, under the ethical imperative. Thus the latter by no means falls out; it only gains the new meaning of *obedience* under God." (Bultmann, "Das Problem der Ethik," p. 195; cf. idem, *Theology of the New Testament*, 1:332 f.

6a. Wendland, *Ethik des Neuen Testaments*, p. 87, collapses this distinction by asserting that "the Spirit is in unity with God's will."

7. Cf. Hans Dieter Betz, *Nachfolge und Nachahmung Jesu Christi im Neuen Testament*, Beiträge zur historischen Theologie, 37 (Tübingen, 1967), p. 181.

infrequently in Paul's letters—it normally functions in the same way as a tenet of holy law. In 1 Cor. 7:10 f. Paul brings in a saying of the Lord (not some principle) as his authority for arguing against divorce and in 1 Cor. 9:14 as justifying the right of an apostle to receive support from his churches. The clearest example of the fact that sayings of the Lord function in the same way as tenets of holy law is 1 Cor. 14:37 f. Here Paul announces that he is going to give a "commandment of the Lord,"[8] and then he gives a tenet of holy law—"If anyone does not know, he is not known."[9] Thus one sees that a saying of the Lord having ethical relevance is relevant directly, absolutely, and arbitrarily, just as is the case with the tenets of holy law.[10] Although these sayings of the Lord do not follow the form of the tenets of holy law (with the exception of 1 Cor. 14:37 f.) and thus do not put forward the eschatological judgment directly, that is very likely nevertheless involved; for Paul views the Lord who gives the sayings (i.e., which also occur in the synoptic tradition) as the same Lord who gives the tenets of holy law—that is, as the one who is coming soon.

Paul's ethics seems to be related to Matthew's in yet another way, and that is in the systematic placing of the command to love at the core of the ethics. Matthew, as has been seen, does this by

8. Admittedly, no synoptic passage containing such a statement exists. But Paul probably did not mean that the "commandment of the Lord" came from the synoptic tradition. In fact, he probably would not have understood the distinction involved (what *only* the earthly Jesus said). What we rather see in 1 Cor. 14:37 f. is that Paul did not make the distinction earthly Jesus/risen Lord where commandments were concerned; rather, he viewed all commandments of the Lord to be equally binding, i.e., absolutely binding. Thus Paul would likely not have distinguished between tenets of holy law, as in 1 Cor. 3:17, and sayings of the Lord, as in 1 Cor. 9:14.

9. Conzelmann, *an die Korinther*, p. 290, seems to have missed the connection and puzzles over how Paul could consider v. 38 a saying of the Lord.

10. This is apparently also seen by Conzelmann, *an die Korinther*, p. 144, who states, "The orders of the historical Jesus are also those of the exalted one." Three other passages designated clearly by Paul as sayings of the Lord appear in his writings. In 1 Thess. 4:15 he cites a saying of the Lord in support of his imminent eschatology (a direct ethical significance does not seem to be involved in this occurrence), and he gives the words of institution for the Lord's Supper in 1 Cor. 11:23–26. Since the latter passage describes in the third person what Jesus did and said, it cannot seriously be considered to be something Jesus himself said. Yet Paul says that the passage comes "from the Lord" (v. 23), and it is followed by an ethical admonition (1 Cor. 11:27–34), which seems to be further evidence of Paul's proclivity for employing sayings of the Lord in the same way as tenets of holy law. Rom. 13:8 f., "Love your neighbor as yourself," also functions ethically, and probably also in the same way as a tenet of holy law, i.e., arbitrarily. The difference is that Paul has made of *this* command an ethical principle. Cf. further below.

understanding the love commandment as principle of interpretation, as the guide used to turn the old law into the new. Paul also
relates the love commandment to the Torah. In Rom. 13:9 Paul
cites the saying of the Lord,[11] "Love your neighbor as yourself,"
and then concludes (v. 10b), "*Agapē* is the fulness of the law."
This does not become principle of interpretation for Paul, however, as for Matthew; rather, Paul's meaning is clearly that whoever loves does not do evil *(to kakon)* to his neighbor (Rom.
13:10a), i.e., whatever laws there may be (v. 9) *are summed up*
(anakephalaioutai) in the love commandment.

In noting the material difference between Rom. 13:8 f. and the
position taken by Matthew, one should observe at the same time
what seems to be a close formal similarity. In Rom. 13:9 Paul lists
four commandments from the Decalogue of Exod. 20 roughly the
same as those given in Matt. 19:18 par. The order Paul gives is
the same as that of Luke 18:20 for the first three of the four prohibitions: adultery, murder, stealing. Mark 10:19 has murder,
adultery, stealing (the order of the Masoretic text), and this order
is followed by Matthew. Neither of these is the Septuagintal order,
where one finds (Exod. 20:13–15) adultery, stealing, murder. The
three synoptic Gospels, however, agree with the Masoretic text
and the Septuagint (Exod. 20:16) in placing bearing false witness
as the fourth prohibition after the three others. Paul places in
fourth position the prohibition that follows bearing false witness
in Exodus—coveting (desiring). Thus, the synoptic Gospels and
Paul agree in general on a list of prohibitions from the ethical

11. That Paul quotes Jesus here and not Lev. 19:18 directly is of course a point
that may be debated. Furnish, *Theology and Ethics in Paul*, p. 57, argues against
"Rom. 13:8 ff." being a quotation of the saying of the Lord on the grounds of formal
differences between the quotation here and in Mark 12:28 ff. par. and of rabbinic
parallels. Two observations, however, would seem to weigh in favor of seeing a
quotation of a saying of the Lord in Rom. 13:8 f. and Gal. 5:14. One is the use of
the term *logos*, "saying," both in Rom. 13:9 and in Gal. 5:14. This is the term
Paul uses in 1 Thess. 4:15 to introduce a saying generally recognized to be a quotation of a dominical saying, although for this quotation "convincing parallels from
synoptic sayings are not to be found" (ibid., p. 52). In 1 Thess. 4:15 Paul specifically
employs the term "saying of the Lord [*logos kyriou*]." Admittedly, he does not
elsewhere use just this term to introduce a recognized quotation of the Lord, but
he never uses *logos* to designate a quotation from Scripture. Thus, the use of *logos*
to designate the form of the love commandment in Rom. 13:9 and Gal. 5:14 may
well point to a conscious quotation of a dominical saying. The second observation
on the side of viewing Rom. 13:8 f. as a quotation of a dominical saying regards
the parallel between Rom. 13:8 f. and Matt. 19:18 f. (overlooked by Furnish), on
which see further below.

Decalogue. Paul agrees in order with Luke but disagrees with all the synoptic Gospels in his choice of the fourth prohibition, and, in their choice of the fourth prohibition, the synoptic Gospels are closer to Exodus than is Paul. One may further note that the three synoptic Gospels add a fifth (for Mark sixth?) commandment from the Decalogue, honoring father and mother, which in Exodus precedes the other four (Exod. 20:12). Paul does not include this commandment. After the list, however, *both Matthew and Paul include the command to love the neighbor as oneself.* Further, Paul is yet closer to Matthew in using *ou* with the future for the four prohibitions (which is the form the Septuagint uses), whereas Mark and Luke employ the prohibitive aorist subjunctive, which is better Greek. One might explain Matthew's use of *ou* plus future as the result of his having referred to the Septuagint, but why did he not then put the order right, i.e., in the same order as the Septuagint? A better explanation seems to be that Matthew has conflated another tradition of these commandments with the tradition before him in Mark 10:19. Since Paul agrees with Matthew both in the grammatical form of the prohibitions and in the adding of the commandment to love one's neighbor, it is reasonable to assume that the other tradition utilized by Matthew is present in an earlier form in Rom. 13:8 f. Thus one may see again, in a most interesting way, how much the tradition of the sayings of the Lord known to Paul is like that which makes up a considerable part of Matthew's special tradition. This similarity exists particularly in *ethical* sayings; yet, the use to which Paul and Matthew put these ethical sayings is altogether different.

To say, as Paul does, that *agapē* is the fullness of the law (Rom. 13:10) is to make an eschatological statement. That is true in the first case because for Paul it is impossible to fulfill the law in the old aeon—the "present evil aeon" (Gal. 1:4)—of man's sinfulness (cf. Gal. 3:10–12). If anyone fulfills the law—even in the Pauline way, even in the way of loving and thereby carrying out the fundamental demand of the law, without in the first instance intending to fulfill the law (but only to love)—if anyone fulfills the law even in this way he is no longer in the here and now but in the coming aeon of God's righteousness. Furthermore, *agapē* is itself an eschatological reality—that is, it belongs to the coming aeon and not to this. In fact, that may be more true for *agapē* than for any other reality Paul discusses; for, in the last verses of 1 Cor. 13 (vv. 8b–13), Paul explains that even the characteristic marks of Christian existence in this life (knowledge, prophecy, and even faith and hope) will cease to exist in the coming aeon. Yet *agapē* will not cease; it belongs *as such* to the coming aeon.[12]

If 1 Cor. 13:8b–13 shows that *agapē* belongs to the coming aeon and is in this sense eschatological, the preceding verses (1 Cor. 13:4–8a) reveal *agapē* to be eschatological in another sense—that is, qualitatively. As Karl Barth so correctly observed,[13] the description of *agapē* in these verses goes far beyond a description of human existence, even of justified human existence. 1 Cor. 13:4–8a, with its list of negatives, describes what man is not. Thus, in the qualitative sense alone, Paul understands *agapē* to be eschatological—that is, transcendent. This transcendence of *agapē* is also understood by Paul Ramsey, who realizes that *agapē* permits *"absolutely everything"* while at the same time commanding *"absolutely everything."*[14] That will be correct. *Agapē* demands nothing and everything. Just in this absolute ethical dimension, however, it would seem to become quite clear that we are dealing with an eschatological reality; for he of whom absolutely everything can be commanded belongs no longer to this life.

Yet Paul commands love in the present. If that command is only implied in Rom. 13:9, it is made explicit in 1 Cor. 14:1, "pursue love." How can these things be reconciled: a belief that no one can fulfill the law in this life, that *agapē* belongs to the coming aeon, and the command to love and in that way to fulfill the law? A discussion of the relation of the imperative to the indicative in Paul's thought will perhaps make that clear.

The indicative dimension of Paul's theology involves the state-

12. For a fuller discussion of this point and extensive treatment of literature dealing with 1 Cor. 13, see my previous article on the subject, "First Corinthians 13. Its Interpretation Since the First World War," *Interpretation* 20 (1966): 159–87.

13. Karl Barth, *The Resurrection of the Dead*, p. 85.

14. Paul Ramsey, *Basic Christian Ethics* (New York, 1950), p. 89. The presentation of *agapē* is somewhat distorted by Ramsey, who discusses it only as ethical norm. In reality, *agapē* becomes ethically compelling only as its indicative dimension implies an imperative. On this, see further below.

ment (2 Cor. 5:17) that "if anyone is in Christ, he is [or there is]
a new creation. The old things have passed away; behold, new
things have come to be." That means that the coming aeon of
God's righteousness has become present reality. Yet the new age
has not become *effective* reality for man, even the man of faith,
since man is still in bondage to—that is, is limited by—the old
aeon, which has not yet ceased to exist.[15] Thus the Christian finds
himself in an overlapping time problem of staggering proportions.[16] Paul's way of stating this overlap is to say that "we were
saved in hope" (Rom. 8:24) or that "(we) were justified by faith"
(Rom. 5:1). Similarly, he can refer to this paradoxical position of
the Christian as one in which the Christian has "the first-fruit of
the Spirit" (Rom. 8:23); or he can reason that crucifixion-and-
resurrection—viewed by Paul as *one* event—is present now as
crucifixion, the resurrection aspect of the event being still out-
standing (Rom. 6:3–8).[17] Thus it is a commonplace of Pauline
theology that the Christian, in his present existence, is not in fact
righteous objectively viewed, but rather, in faith, has his right-

15. Robert C. Tannehill, in *Dying and Rising with Christ*, correctly relates this
"already but not yet" aspect of Paul's eschatology to his view of dying and rising
with Christ (passim, particularly pp. 76 f.). There can be no doubt that, as Tannehill suggests (pp. 82, 103, 128), the relation of imperative to indicative is also
predicated upon Paul's concept of dying and rising with Christ; the indicative is
the resurrection side of the premise, the imperative is the crucifixion side. If Paul
can refer to the death of Christ by saying, "He loved me and gave himself for me"
(Gal. 2:20), and then command love, the love is a manifestation of the crucifixion,
i.e., love involves dying to the present evil aeon. Thus Tannehill observes with
acumen that "God has already conquered death, not by abolishing it (this is still
future) but by commandeering it for his own purposes" (p. 77). The imperative
means, then, that one should "allow God's lordship over you to manifest itself in
your will and actions" (p. 82). One will only have to add that Paul means to admit
no qualification of that absolute imperative.

16. Herbert Preisker, in *Das Ethos des Urchristentums*, p. 175, observes that this
concept of being, in a certain sense, already in the new time of God's righteousness
makes Paul's position look, at first glance, like the general stoic notion of being
detached from the world. This, of course, reminds one of the withdrawal from the
world found in Mark and Luke. Yet Preisker correctly notes that the "motivation"
for the "detachment" is different in Paul's thought from what it is in Stoicism.
But the "motivation" is in fact so different that Paul is not at all led to propose
withdrawal from the world, and in fact specifically rejects such a position, cf.
1 Cor. 5:9 f. Wendland, *Ethik des Neuen Testaments*, p. 51, holds on to the notion
of being "between the times." On the other hand, he also thinks (ibid., p. 88) that
Paul's ethical commands can be fulfilled because the Christian has received new life.

17. It obviously goes beyond the purposes of this work to present here any fuller
explanation of Paul's theology of salvation. A thorough treatment of the whole of
Paul's theology may of course be found in Bultmann, *Theology of the New Testament*, vol. 1, pp. 187–352. Cf. further Furnish, *Theology and Ethics*, pp. 112–206,
and Tannehill, *Dying and Rising*.

eousness attributed to him by God.[18] That is the indicative side of salvation. Obviously, another way of stating this aspect of the indicative would be to say that the indicative is lacking something, i.e., its culmination, fulfillment, completion (*to teleion*, 1 Cor. 13:10).[19] Thus the fact that the person declared righteous still exists as unrighteous (*asebēs*, Rom. 4:5) leads Paul to call at the same time for that which is reckoned to one. If the Christian is one who has been accounted righteous, then the Christian should be righteous; if a Christian is one who loves, then a Christian should love. This relation of imperative to indicative is also clear from Gal. 5:22 f., where Paul names *agapē* first in the list of the aspects of the "fruit of the Spirit"; for the function of the concluding statement there (v. 25, "If we live by the Spirit, let us also follow the Spirit") of the imperative in the indicative does not *add the imperative onto* the foregoing verses; rather, the imperative is implied in them already. What else could be the point of listing the "works of the flesh" (vv. 19–21), adding that no one who "does such things will inherit the Kingdom of God," and then giving a catalog of the "fruit of the Spirit" (vv. 22 f.), if not to admonish laying aside works of the flesh and taking up the fruit of the Spirit? The function of verse 25 is then not to present the imperative, but rather to guard against the misunderstanding that inheriting the Kingdom is *dependent upon* one's exhibiting love, joy, peace, etc., i.e., dependent upon the carrying out of the imperative. Confusing as it may be in view of the existence of the imperative, Paul does not view God's salvation as being dependent

18. This point is made clearly enough by Bultmann, *Theology of the New Testament*, vol. 1, p. 276. Furnish, *Theology and Ethics*, pp. 151–53, argues that this "forensic" view of justification is somewhat untrue to Paul, since it seems to result in criminals being released. Furnish prefers the analogy of juvenile court, where an "acquitted offender" is placed under the guidance of the court and given training in how to be a proper citizen. In this way, argues Furnish, the court acts to reconcile the acquitted offender to society. Although Furnish goes on at this point to discuss the relation of sanctification to justification (pp. 153–57), concluding that sanctification cannot mean the "*development* or *actualization* of justification," it is difficult to see how his analogy avoids allowing one to think that the offender merits his justification, even if that occurs only ex post facto. In insisting that justification actually changes the justified one (p. 151), Furnish has come close to rejecting a cardinal point of Pauline theology, that the Christian remains, prior to the eschaton at least, a sinner justified by God—that is, Furnish seems not to take radically enough the objective character of justification.

19. Conzelmann, *an die Korinther*, p. 267, relates *to teleion* to the Parousia and completion. Cf. further Otto Merk, *Handeln aus Glauben*, p. 40.

on man's righteousness; rather, it is the one who *has been justified* who falls under the derived imperative to live in keeping with that existence which God has imputed to him. Thus the indicative always calls forth the imperative, thus Paul always finds the imperative implied in the indicative—"always" because the indicative always states what man is not, i.e., what God imputes to him.[20]

Thus, it may now be seen that it is *because of his belief in an imminent eschaton* that Paul can command righteousness now of those who are not in fact righteous but who have been accounted so.[21] With respect to *agapē*, Paul does this at the end of 1 Cor. 13. Here, as has been seen above, after arguing (1 Cor. 13:1–8a) for the greater advantage of *agapē* over all other manifestations of Christian existence, Paul points out (vv. 8b–13) how all other aspects of Christian existence in the here and now will cease when "the perfect" (*to teleion*, i.e., the complete) comes. Love alone carries over into the new aeon from Christian existence in this aeon. But that means that *agapē* alone, of all aspects of Christian existence now, designates the quality of the coming aeon! Yet Paul concludes (1 Cor. 14:1), "pursue *agapē*." Presumably, Paul views the new aeon as present, as breaking in, where *agapē* exists. The Christian is for him not merely "between the times" but rather in two times.[22] At one and the same time, the Christian is in the old aeon of sin and death, in which the fulfilling of the law

20. It may occur to someone that the imperative does not logically follow from the indicative. Apparently, that occurred already to some of Paul's earliest hearers. The indicative of the granting of justification and the freedom connected with it apparently led some Corinthian Christians to think that they had already been filled, had already become rich, and already—apart from Paul—reigned (1 Cor. 4:8); cf. Hans Lietzmann, *An die Korinther 1, 2*, HNT, 9 (Tübingen, 1949⁴), p. 19. That the indicative of justification, "rightwising," carries with it for Paul the imperative, be righteous! (i.e., love!) reveals that Paul recognized the disparity between the indicative and the actual existence of those persons to whom the indicative applied.

21. The very thorough work of Merk also details this fact, except for one important aspect—that is, that Merk has overlooked the importance of *imminence* in the eschatological grounding. In his conclusion, Merk finally collapses Paul's eschatology into the *dialectic* of the certainty of the coming of God's righteousness. See Merk, *Handeln aus Glauben*, pp. 242 f.

22. In his posthumously published *The Kingdom of God and Primitive Christianity*, Albert Schweitzer correctly noted (p. 167) that love is not for Paul ethics "directed toward entry into the Kingdom. . . . For him it is proof that we are in the Kingdom." Schweitzer nevertheless continued (p. 168) to insist that this was *Interimsethik*.

is impossible, and—in faith and hope—in the new aeon of God's righteousness, where the fulfilling of the law, i.e., *agapē* is an accomplished fact. In his bondage to the flesh, the Christian cannot love; but, in the new existence granted to him in faith, and which is shortly to be actualized by God's coming, he can love or, at least, be commanded to love—that is, to attest the existence which he knows, in faith, to be his. Paul's position on this matter may appear to be nonsense; and, in fact, it becomes so when the eschatology loses its edge of imminence. That the relation of imperative to indicative just described is inextricably bound together with Paul's imminent eschatology can be seen still better by an analysis of the immediate context of Rom. 13:8–10, i.e., Rom. 12:1–15:7.

It is generally acknowledged that Paul turns, in Rom. 12:1, to a discussion that quite consciously intends to be instructive regarding what a Christian is to do. This is not to say that a kerygmatic section (chaps. 1–11) is followed by a didactic section, or a theological by a practical section; for chapters 1–11 are not without *applicatio* (with chap. 12 cf. particularly 6:12–23), whereas chapters 12 ff. are unashamedly theological (see particularly 14:23). But Paul does intend, beginning at 12:1, now explicitly to tell the Romans how Christians should live—or, perhaps better, be.

Paul's opening covering statement, "Present your bodies [selves] as a living and holy sacrifice, and one pleasing to God," is quickly followed by a clarification: Be transformed. This transformation is then immediately said to be a renewing of the mind, but a renewing of the mind in a definite sense, the sense of being able to assent to God's will—that is, to what is good and pleasing (i.e., pleasing to God)[23] and perfect. That is to say, the Christian is to do the good, the perfect, and what is pleasing to God. That is God's will. (Could God's will be any less?) The Christian can do this, however, only if his mind has been renewed so that he can assent to God's will, i.e., only if he has been transformed. That itself is, in turn, what is involved in presenting oneself as a living, holy, and pleasing-to-God sacrifice. In these two verses, then, Paul obviously encourages an existence that can belong only to the coming aeon.

23. Cf. also Otto Michel, *Der Brief an die Römer*, p. 291.

With verse 3 Paul begins to explain more in detail what the
formulation of verses 1 f. means. He does this first by reiterating
(apparently) his discussion in 1 Cor. 12 and 14 about charismata,
the highest of which is prophecy. Thus Rom. 12:3–8 seems briefly
to summarize the argument there. Verse 9, then, sets in abruptly
with *agapē*; but this is not abrupt at all if one recalls 1 Cor. 12–14,
for love was the subject there and precisely the climax of the
argument (chap. 13). What follows, down to Rom. 13:10, is then
a clarification about *agapē*, about what it means that a Christian
loves. Rom. 12:9–13:10 may thus be seen as a single coordinated
unit explaining what *agapē* is, or giving in detail what one may
call the "manifestations" of love, and heightening the motivation
to do God's will. (One is reminded by Rom. 12:9–16 of the list in
1 Cor. 13:4–8a). Rom. 12:9–13:10 is in no way disconnected from
12:1 f., for Paul makes it perfectly plain at the outset that non-
hypocritical, i.e., genuine, "true" love means a rejection of evil
and a being bound to the good—that is, to the good at the end of
verse 2, the good that is God's will. If one is, however, to cling to
the perfect good, the good that is pleasing to God (which appears
now to be the interpretation of *agapē*—or vice versa), then naturally all evil is to be "renounced" (v. 9), and one is to "return no
one evil for evil" (v. 17). In fact, the Christian is enjoined to
"conquer evil with the good."[24]

After the general rubric given in Rom. 12:9, Paul then explains, of course, in some detail in Rom. 12:10–20(19) what patterns
of behavior are involved in the general statement of verse 9, in
"true" love, in "being bound to the good," in conquering "evil
with the good." Paul does not here seek to list specific actions;
how could that be done without reference to a specific context?
But the list is by no means abstract. It is here irrelevant from
what sources Paul has drawn the specifics of this list; verse 14
certainly reminds one of the Q saying found in varying form in
Matt. 5:44 and Luke 6:28, and verse 15 is somewhat less reminiscent of Luke 6:21b and 25b. The *underlying criteria*, however,
seem to be more determinative for the specifics of the list than is

24. The connection between "the good" of 12:2 and 12 and the *agapē* of 12:9 is
probably further reflected in Paul's choice of the word *agapētoi*, beloved (of God),
in v. 19—just in case anyone might be inclined to overlook the fact that the discussion about the good was at the same time a discussion about love.

provenance. That is to say, Paul seems to be explaining Rom. 12:9 by setting down in Rom. 12:10–20 a list of middle axioms predicated upon certain general and fundamental norms. Perhaps one should say "presuppositions" rather than "norms"; for there is clearly one norm here, what is called *philadelphia* or *philostorgia* (v. 10), always for Paul the primary mode of *agapē* in Christian existence. The other presupposition, however, is hardly what one would normally label "ethical norm"; it is rather the eschatological motif—Paul's view that the new aeon of God's righteousness was fast approaching and was in certain ways already present. This comes most clearly to expression, in 12:9–20, in the "hope" of verse 12 and in the concluding expression of eschatological judgment in verses 19 f., but in fact every mode of conduct given in the list would seem to be applicable given one—or both—of the two presuppositions, brotherly love and imminent eschatology. The eschatological motif is surely prominent in the whole of verse 12, not only in the hope, and even the manifestation of *agapē* as *philadelphia/philostorgia* is itself a manifestation of the presence of the eschaton (i.e., a fruit of the Spirit, cf. Gal. 5:22–26).

When one now sees that Rom. 12:9 ff. intends to explain God's will for man as *agapē*/doing the good,[25] then Rom. 13:1–7 becomes more intelligible. This passage is not essentially a discussion about rulers at all, but about the good, as becomes clear in verse 3 (the rulers are a fright to bad works but not to good).[26] Why is one, after all, to "be subject to the powers that be" (v. 1)? Because they promote the good! As verse 4 says, an "authority" "is God's minister for the purpose of getting you to do the good." Paul thus argues in this verse that two "encouragements to the

25. Cf. also Furnish, *Theology and Ethics*, p. 228. Michel, *Brief an die Römer*, pp. 300 f., probably mistakenly considers the juxtaposition of *agapē* and the good in Rom. 12:9–21 to be the result of bringing in catchwords from different paraenetic traditions; but that Paul identifies the two here Michel sees clearly enough (p. 308).

26. Since this is the case, it is unimportant whether the *exousiai* or *archontes* are earthly or heavenly rulers. The most reasonable position is that Paul is referring to earthly rulers (as the argument below tends to attest). The opinion that the *exousiai* are heavenly powers, an opinion now most prominently associated with the name of Oscar Cullmann, has been soundly refuted by Hans von Campenhausen, "Zur Auslegung von Röm 13," in *Festschrift Alfred Bertholet zum 80. Geburtstag*, pp. 97–113; so also Gerhard Delling, *Römer 13, 1–7 innerhalb der Briefe des Neuen Testaments* (Berlin, 1962), pp. 20–34, and August Strobel, "Zum Verständnis von Rm 13," *ZNW* 47 (1956): 67–93.

good" exist.[27] The one is the will of God, which is love, i.e., the good. The other is the "authorities," who may execute "wrath" upon "the evil doer." Thus there are two reasons (v. 5) for "being subject"—which equals, of course, doing the good (cf. v. 4 again). One is the wrath of the "authorities," which will fall upon one's head if one does *not* do the good; the other is conscience, i.e., that evaluative aspect of mind now functioning in its "renewed" (12:2) capacity.[28]

Paul may now sum up the section that began at 12:9 by returning to the principle. What is it, after all, to do the good?[29] It is, simply stated, to "owe no one anything except to love one another" (13:8). That is what the whole law intends. The famous and often misquoted statement of Augustine would thus appear to be justified: *Dilige, et quod vis fac.*[30] If one understands what *agapē* is—that is, as explained in 12:9 ff.—and if one then *loves*, that is in fact doing the whole law, for "love is the fulness of the law" (13:10). It should be observed that Paul does not derive the understanding of *agapē* as the fulfilling of the Torah from this saying of the Lord quoted here at the end of the argument.

27. C. K. Barrett, *A Commentary on the Epistle to the Romans*, translates Rom. 13:4 (ad loc.), "For he is God's servant, appointed to promote what is good." Michel, *Brief an die Römer*, p. 318, insists on viewing the good here as something different from the good that equals *agapē* in 12:9–21 (cf. above, p. 58, n. 24); but such an interpretation robs the passage of its relevance to the argument.

28. That this is the role of v. 5 is clearly seen by Rudolf Bultmann in his *Theology of the New Testament*, vol. 1, pp. 218 f. Cf. further the whole discussion of conscience there, pp. 216–20. Bultmann seems to get the cart before the horse, however, in finding in Rom. 13:5 two reasons for "obedience to the government." There appear rather to be two motivations—one of them obedience to the government—given for *doing the good*. Barrett, *Romans*, pp. 246 f., correctly and succinctly notes, "It is necessary to be in subjection, not only through fear of God's wrath, but also for conscience sake." The point is also exactly seen by Herbert Preisker, *Das Ethos des Urchristentums*, p. 87. Cf. further Michel, *Brief an die Römer*, p. 319.

29. Michel, *Brief an die Römer*, p. 312, considers Rom. 13:1–7 to be an "independent insertion." Yet he also (inconsistently) sees (p. 314) that the passage is related back to 12:1–2. That Rom. 13:1–7 could be an insertion is completely ruled out by von Campenhausen, *Festschrift Bertholet*, pp. 109 f., who shows a close parallelism between 1 Thess. 5:1–15 and Rom. 12 and 13. The argument proceeds in opposite directions in the two passages, 1 Thess. 5:1–12 generally paralleling Rom. 13 and 1 Thess. 5:14 f. giving briefly essentially the same argument as in Rom. 12, but the pattern of the argument is in both cases the same! Käsemann also fails to understand the relation of Rom. 13:1–7 to its context, arguing (Käsemann, "Principles of the Interpretation of Romans 13," *New Testament Questions of Today*, p. 199) that these verses "cannot be directly associated" with 13:8–10, nor with vv. 11 ff.

30. To be found in J. P. Migne, ed., *Patrologiae cursus completus*, Series Latina, vol. 35 (Paris, 1845), col. 2033.

Rather, the argument leads to this point naturally, for the law of course intended to be an expression of God's will. The more basic category is, therefore, doing God's will. Paul proceeds to explain what doing God's will is, in Rom. 12:1 ff., on the basis of the Christian principle of *agapē*. If by loving, however, one in fact does God's will, then one may say that one has also fulfilled the law, for the law also explains God's will.[31]

Has Paul not in fact now said too much? Is it really possible to fulfill the law, even in the way Paul has set out? Has not Paul himself even hinted, by the *ei dynaton* ("if it is possible") of 12:18, that he knows that no one can fulfill the law—even in his way?[32] Of course, one would have to add to these questions the qualification, "in this life." What is then the point of going into such detail to encourage Christians to do God's will and to explain how they may do so? If in *this* aeon one cannot do God's will, but only in the *next*, is not Rom. 12:1–13:10 just so much wasted papyrus? It is to this problem which is posed in the whole section, Rom. 12:1–13:10, and which becomes most critical in the last three verses, that Paul now addresses himself in 13:11–14: In taking it upon oneself to do God's will, one must "observe the time." IT IS ALREADY THE HOUR TO GET UP! "Salvation is nearer than when we believed. The night has advanced, the day has drawn nigh" (vv. 11 f.). Since it is now the time of the dawn of the day of God's righteousness, the long awaited day, the day in which one *will* be able to fulfill the law, to love, to do the good *without* the limitation of the *ei dynaton*, for that reason it is time to "put off the works of darkness" and to "clothe oneself with the weapons of light" (v. 12)—that is, the imminence of the eschaton makes the imperative possible.[33]

---

31. It is interesting to note that Paul refers to loving "one another" and "the other [person]" (v. 9) until he cites the saying of the Lord, after which he uses the term "neighbor" (v. 10). Thus Paul seems to understand "neighbor" to mean first the Christian brother, but secondly any other person. Note further 1 Thess. 3:12.

32. Cf. also Preisker, *Das Ethos des Urchristentums*, p. 184.

33. This is also the case in 1 Cor. 7:29–31, the famous *hōs mē* (as though not) passage, as Wolfgang Schrage, "Die Stellung zur Welt bei Paulus, Epiktet und in der Apokalyptik," *ZThK* 61 (1964): 125–54, has made clear. Schrage states concisely (p. 149), "The *paragei* [is passing away] is the basis of the *hōs mē*, it does not follow therefrom. Only because the world is coming to an end . . . does the *hōs mē* have its meaning." The attempt of André Feuillet, "Les fondements de la morale chrétienne d'après l'Épitre aux Romains," *RevThom* 70 (1970): 373 f., to explain

Now that the eschatological orientation is clear, now that Paul
has explained how one is justified in taking eschatological existence upon oneself, i.e., in accepting the love commandment (the
night is advanced), he proceeds in chapter 14 to attempt to explain Christian life more in detail—that is, to show how concern
for one's fellow man may be related to a *particular* situation.
Again he seems to fall back on 1 Corinthians (presumably because
he has no personal acquaintance with the Roman church and
reasons that its problems would be similar to those at Corinth).
Rom. 14 is very reminiscent of the two discussions in 1 Corinthians about the problems of eating, particularly 1 Cor. 8:8–13
and 10:24–31.[34] Rom. 14:20a, 21 is in fact almost a quotation of
1 Cor. 8:13. Thus Paul seems to have sought to show in chapter
14, paradigmatically (and in reliance on 1 Corinthians), how one
moves from the middle axioms given in 12:9–20 to specific paraenesis.

After this discussion in chapter 14, the whole section is then
concluded by 15:1–6, with a terse christological summary in 15:7.
The principle of 13:8 is picked up again in 15:1 with the "we
owe" and related to the particulars of chapter 14 by formulating
the obligation in terms of strong/weak. That the opening of
chapter 15 reaches back to 13:8—that is, back to the fundamental
ethical principle—is further seen in the use of "please the neighbor" in 15:2. However one is to translate the double prepositional
phrase in verse 2, *eis to agathon pros oikodomēn*, it is clear that
this phrase intends to qualify "pleasing the neighbor" in the
sense of the foregoing discussion in chapters 12–14; *eis to agathon*
(for the good) recalls the general context of concern for one's
fellow man, i.e., the good (Rom. 12:9–13:10), and *pros oikodomēn*
(unto edification) has the nearer context in view, the supportive
character of one's relationship with one's fellows (Rom. 14). In
other words, the command of the Lord, *agapēsete ton plēsion* (you
shall love your neighbor), has in effect been translated in the discussion ensuing from 13:8 as *aresete tōi plēsion* (you shall please

---

away the imminent eschatology in Rom. 13:11–14 as being only the triumph of the
Christian world over the pagan world, because the sins mentioned in v. 13 are
pagan sins, is certainly incorrect, although Feuillet *does* see the integral relation
between vv. 11 ff. and the foregoing.

34. Cf. also Michel, *Brief an die Römer*, p. 289.

your neighbor) *eis to agathon pros oikodomēn,* which Paul now says explicitly. The christological grounding for this way of putting the fundamental ethical imperative, which is tersely summarized in verse 7, is explained in verses 3–6: If anyone is in Christ (and not fleshly), then he should exemplify that reality in his existence. (With Rom. 15:5 f., one should compare particularly Phil. 2:1–11.) Yet to be in Christ is eschatological existence, eschatological reality; hence, as becomes clear with the "hope" of verse 4 (expressed again twice in 15:13),[35] to love, to do the good, to support and help the weak express the existence for which one hopes. Paul can command (or enjoin) such existence now because —and *only* because—the hoped for existence is about to be actualized by God.

As the above analysis has demonstrated, *agapē* as commandment[36] has its validity, for Paul, in the existence of *agapē* as transcendent, i.e., eschatological. Paul means that primarily temporally, as has been seen. But Paul for the first time puts *agapē* as command in a new dimension. *Agapē* is for Paul not *just* God's requirement in view of his coming righteousness (as with Jesus), but it is also a qualitative designation of transcendence where the Christian already begins to live; for precisely the central designation of the eschaton by a *quality—agapē—*shows that Paul has made a step in the direction of understanding transcendence qualitatively rather than temporally. This may well be a more or less unconscious step, since Paul normally holds strongly to temporal transcendence—that is, to his imminent eschatology.[37] Nevertheless, Paul alone, of all the New Testament writers (and Jesus) yet considered, offers a possibility for an ethics that is not essentially grounded in an imminent eschatology. Of course, Paul only offers the *possibility* for such an ethics; he does not present it himself. For Paul, *agapē* designates the *eschaton*; he would not

35. Cf. also Michel, *Brief an die Römer,* pp. 356 f.
36. Or as ethical orientation, or as "*characteristic* Christian style of life" (Furnish, *Theology and Ethics,* p. 241).
37. It seems to be precisely this point that was recognized by Bultmann when he argued, against Barth (see above), that 1 Cor. 13 was really a more adequate conceptualization of the subject matter that is also present in chap. 15 (which deals with the resurrection)—that is, Bultmann agreed with Barth that eschatology was also the subject matter of chap. 13 but argued that it was presented in chap. 13 in its meaning for present existence. Cf. Rudolf Bultmann, "Karl Barth, 'Die Auferstehung der Toten,'" in *Glauben und Verstehen,* vol. 1 (Tübingen, 1933), pp. 52, 64.

have understood separating the two. God's coming Kingdom was for him absolute certainty. It only happens that the Kingdom could best be designated by the terms righteousness and love (with the latter giving a more specific content to the former). But Paul has, in viewing transcendence also qualitatively, offered a live ethical alternative for any time, even a time that knows that it does not stand before God's imminent coming. One would seem to be able to say, without being untrue to the thrust of Paul's statements about *agapē*, that, because transcendent reality is *agapē*, one should "pursue *agapē*." Defining the details of such an ethics would be as difficult today as for Paul, so that a situation ethics would appear to be unavoidable.[38]

Such a position would also overcome, at least in part, the problem that the ethical demands presented in the New Testament are (as far as has been seen up until now) for Christians only. Of course, it would still have to be believed that transcendence is *agapē*, but such a statement of faith would likely have an appeal far beyond the confines of the other normal specifics of Christian faith.

Aside from the tenets of holy law, which function arbitrarily, Paul does give many specific ethical admonitions that seem to be coordinated under the command to love. A general discussion of these will suffice for our purposes here.[39]

38. The position of Erich Dinkler, "Zum Problem der Ethik bei Paulus. Rechtsnahme und Rechtsversicht (1. Kor. 6, 1–11)," *ZThK* 49 (1952): 186, that Paul himself actually *proposes* a situation ethics is attractive and is certainly consistent with Paul's position when it is presented in the abstract. The only problem is that Paul all too often employs another principle when he deals with a particular situation.

39. An excellent and extensive analysis of Paul's individual ethical exhortations is given by Wolfgang Schrage, *Die konkreten Einzelgebote in der paulinischen Paränese. Ein Beitrag zur neutestamentlichen Ethik* (Gütersloh, 1961). This work has the avowed purpose of inquiring "whether, alongside the love commandment, yet other commandments are not also possible, necessary, and binding" (p. 12). After finding that they are, Schrage nevertheless concludes that "all paraenesis is finally example, expression, and sharpening of the love commandment" (p. 269). Schrage seems to err, however, in concluding that Paul's individual exhortations are not thereby "relativized" (p. 269). Of course they are not relativized in Paul's thinking because he foresees no alteration whatever in the context of human existence, due to his imminent eschatology. (Schrage correctly sees the primary function of eschatology in Paul's ethics.) Cf. further Preisker, *Das Ethos des Urchristentums*, pp. 189–92. Preisker, on p. 183, correctly notes that the delay of the eschaton prompts the specific admonitions. This at the same time shows the primary difference between the ethics of Jesus and the ethics of Paul: "Whereas . . . Jesus as prophet only calls into the world what is God's will, without asking how broadly and with what limitation it becomes reality, Paul, as pastor of his congregations, wrestles with life's difficulties and has to make allowances for life." The slogan-like statement of

Paul's many ethical admonitions have a varied background, coming often from the Old Testament, from other Jewish sources, and from Hellenistic popular philosophy, as well as from some other sources.[40] One reason for this ethical eclecticism will be immediately obvious: lacking a body of ethical teaching, Christianity must naturally make use of existing ethical instruction. Yet, may one speculate at all regarding what Paul himself must have thought when appropriating non-Christian ethical instruction for Christian application? Another way of phrasing this question is to ask whether Paul thought that these ethical specifics, derived from Judaism and paganism, were in some way Christianized or took on a Christian cast by his use of them, and if so, in what way.[41] As we saw in Rom. 14 and 15, Paul explained at considerable length how specific ethical action must in some way manifest doing the good to, i.e., loving one's fellow man; and he offered, in 15:2, the translation of the love commandment that each one should "please the neighbor *eis to agathon pros oikodomēn*" (literally, "for the good unto edification"). One will thus very likely be correct in understanding Paul as thinking that *all* the specific ethical admonitions he gives represent manifestations of this basic principle. The Christian is one who "does the good" to his fellow man.

Normally, the way in which one is to do the good is expressed abstractly or in general, even when Paul does so at length.[42] As we have seen, when he essays to give ethical guidance in individual cases, he tends to rely on tenets of holy law or sayings of the Lord (both understood as coming from the Lord and hence functioning

---

Conzelmann, *an die Korinther*, p. 123, that "morals are bourgeois because faith is eschatological" is quite incorrect, as will also be seen in the next chapter. Conzelmann makes the same mistake in his evaluation of Paul in idem, *An Outline of the Theology of the New Testament*, p. 283.

40. Furnish gives a thorough discussion of the sources of Paul's ethical admonitions (Furnish, *Theology and Ethics*, pp. 25–67) and concludes that "Paul . . . does not hesitate to employ current forms, concepts, and standards, even secular ones, already familiar to his readers" (p. 65).

41. Furnish's attempt to answer this question by calling attention to Paul's "concern to be concrete and relevant," his "concern to be inclusive," and his "concern to be persuasive" (Furnish, *Theology and Ethics*, pp. 72–81), not incorrect as far as it goes, does not at all reach the core of the matter.

42. This can especially be seen in the catalogs of "vices and virtues" Paul gives in some places, as in Gal. 5:19–23. Cf. Siegfried Wibbing, *Die Tugend- und Lasterkataloge im Neuen Testament und ihre Traditionsgeschichte unter besonderer Berücksichtigung der Qumran-Texte*, BZNW, 25 (Berlin, 1959), pp. 100, 123.

in the same way). Thus it is difficult to escape the conclusion that Paul is in this way often inconsistent with his own position. He seems to intend that all action should be grounded in the basic principle of doing the good to one's fellow man; yet, when confronted with an actual event calling for some kind of ethical direction, he has a tendency to forget that ground rule and to rule arbitrarily, i.e., by direct revelation from the Lord.[43] If Paul is to be made ethically relevant for today, it would seem to have to be by rejecting this element of his ethics, which is a manifestation pure and simple of imminent eschatology, and by endorsing as accurate the move Paul makes toward understanding transcendence qualitatively and the ethics of *agapē* implied in that understanding.

43. Preisker, *Das Ethos des Urchristentums*, p. 195, sees clearly the danger involved in this inconsistency: "Thus the unity of conduct in the love commandment is . . . endangered by the dissolution into many individual virtues."

IV

THE LATER EPISTLES IN THE

PAULINE TRADITION

Paul was probably the most influential apostle in the early church. After him, others (perhaps in some cases disciples or companions of his) sought to perpetuate this influence in the rapidly changing theology of early Christianity, and for this purpose they used the means that had apparently been so effective for him, the letter. In order to add strength to their ideas, these followers and imitators of Paul wrote under his name (with one exception), sought in other ways to provide in their letters verisimilitude for the claim of Pauline authorship, and followed, with now greater, now less success, the distinctive form of a Pauline letter. These persons were the authors of Colossians, Ephesians, 2 Thessalonians, 1 and 2 Timothy, Titus, and 1 Peter.[1]

Imitating Paul's style, however, and copying his words and phrases did not assure repetition of Paul's theology. Rather, distinctive alterations were introduced into the tradition of Pauline theology. In fact, it may readily be argued that Paul's imitators had no intention of reproducing Paul's theology, which they may have regarded as passé (or misunderstood, which is more likely),

---

1. In general, cf. the discussions of these letters in the standard work by Werner Georg Kümmel, *Introduction to the New Testament*. On 1 Peter as belonging with this group, cf. ibid., p. 297. Kümmel still regards Colossians and 2 Thessalonians as Pauline, in spite of a rather widespread opinion to the contrary (cf. ibid., pp. 187–90, 240–44). More recently, however, the commentary on Colossians by Eduard Lohse seems finally to have resolved the argument regarding that Epistle in favor of non-Pauline authorship. Cf. Eduard Lohse, *Colossians and Philemon*; the evidence is given throughout. On the non-Pauline authorship of 2 Thessalonians, one might cite Herbert Braun, "Zur nachpaulinischen Herkunft des zweiten Thessalonicherbriefes," in *Gesammelte Studien zum Neuen Testament und seiner Umwelt* (Tübingen, 1967), pp. 205–9. That Colossians, Ephesians, 2 Thessalonians, 1 and 2 Timothy, Titus, and 1 Peter are pseudonymous and imitate Paul's style and thought is not to be debated here but rather accepted as an assured result of historical critical scholarship.

but rather employed not only a famous name, but also a well-known style and familiar theological terminology and phraseology in order to make their own points. It is to this later development, stemming from Paul's theology, that we now turn. What happens to the love commandment, the imperative in the indicative, the tenets of holy law in the writings of those Christians who try to make their Epistles look like Paul's?

COLOSSIANS AND EPHESIANS

A quick perusal of these two Epistles or of a concordance will show that the love commandment nowhere appears in either of them. The author of Colossians enjoins his readers to "put on . . . love" (Col. 3:14), "which binds [the virtues listed in vv. 12 f.] together in perfection."[2] (The virtues are mercifulness, goodness, humility, gentleness, endurance, sustaining one another, and forgiving themselves, i.e., one another.) Love is thus no longer at all a radical demand to care for and to do good to one's neighbor. It is rather made here into an over-arching structural element of theology that ties together the several virtues.[3] To be sure, these virtues still for the most part have the neighbor in view, but the emphasis is more on one's own attitude than on a response to the neighbor's need. One thus has the distinct impression that the presence of *agapē* in this list is purely formal. It has lost any definitive character so that the virtues listed do not grow out of love, do not make love definite, but rather are derived from elsewhere, and love is then brought in as the crowning virtue. If one exemplifies all the virtues and loves as well, one will be perfect. In Eduard Lohse's words, "Love is understood as the bond that leads to perfection."[4] That is the meaning of the binding "together in perfection"; but the author of Colossians does not tell us what it means to love.

2. Literally, "the together-bond of perfection"; the genitive is epexegetical, however. and has the meaning given. What is bound together can only be the virtues listed in vv. 12 f. Cf. Walter Bauer, *A Greek-English Lexicon of the New Testament*, trans. William F. Arndt and F. Wilbur Gingrich (Chicago, 1957), *syndesmos* 1.b.

3. Cf. the statement of Herbert Preisker, *Das Ethos des Urchristentums*, p. 199, that "love is . . . not a spirit power that moves man, but a norm that receives legal interpretation." Preisker is referring here in general to the deutero-Paulines, the Catholic Epistles, and the Apostolic Fathers. We see the first steps toward this situation in Colossians and Ephesians.

4. Lohse, *Colossians and Philemon*, p. 149.

What brings about this weakened understanding of the demand to love is the eschatology of the author of Colossians. For Paul, as for Jesus, the radical demand to love was called forth by God's imminent righteousness. The one, however, cannot be maintained without the other; thus, when love is found to have lost its cutting edge, one may well suspect that eschatology has also lost the sharpness of its imminence. That is in fact the case. To be sure, the eschatological setting is not entirely given up for Colossians since the "perfection" of Col. 3:14 will be the final perfection manifested in the eschatological congregation, as likewise the "peace . . . to which you were also called" of verse 15; but the eschatology is turned on its head. Instead of looking ahead to the imminent end time and concluding therefrom that love is commanded, the author of Colossians views the Christian congregation as the place where the new life is to be found—as God's home on earth, so to speak. Thus the Christian is requested to clothe himself in certain attitudes and modes of action befitting Christianity, or, as Col. 3:2 has it, to "consider the things above, not those on the earth." That the author of Colossians can use such phraseology shows how far he has in reality moved from Paul's temporal understanding toward a concept of two realms, more familiar to readers whose heritage was Hellenic and not Jewish.[5] He brings the two-realm understanding into harmony with Paul's understanding of justification and his imperative in the indicative by affirming that the Christian has "been raised with Christ" (3:1), and by adding immediately, "seek the things above."

The truth is, then, that the author of Colossians has made out of Pauline Christianity a saved society, so that the stating of the ethical imperative does not follow consistently from the definition of a Christian. The imperative in the indicative is then, by a tour de force, artificially brought into conjunction with the definition of a Christian as one who has already been raised with Christ. This is accomplished by Col. 3:3, "You have died, but your life has been hidden with Christ in God." That statement has just enough of the Pauline "eschatological reservation" about

---

5. Cf. particularly Lohse, pp. 145, 180; also his remark on pp. 164 f. that the injunction to "watch" in Col. 4:2 is now meant as an everyday thing and not as an eschatological command.

it to allow validity to ethical imperatives. "You have died," verse
3, does not retract "You have been raised," verse 1. It does say,
however, that the resurrection that has already taken place for
the Christian is a secret resurrection, a resurrection that places
one, invisibly, already in the divine sphere, whereas one remains
visibly within the earthly sphere.[6] The purpose, then, for behaving like a Christian in the here and now is, for the author of
Colossians, to bring one's visible existence as much as possible
into harmony with one's invisible resurrection existence. Apparently, not to do so will bring upon one God's wrath (Col. 3:6)
but the secondary reason given for behaving like a Christian—
that Christian behavior marks off the Christian from the non-
Christian (v. 7, "in which even you walked then when you lived
in them")—ought not to be overlooked. That will also be important for our author. That is to say, the question of how one distinguishes the Christian from the non-Christian now seems to
arise, and the author of Colossians seeks to answer that question
by referring to ethics: the non-Christian does those evil things
listed in 3:5–9; the Christian is better—or at least he should be.
If the Christian wants to be perfect, he crowns his virtues with
love.

This same situation also exists in Ephesians, for which Colossians serves as extensive source material.[7] *Agapē* is taken more
fully into account in Ephesians than in Colossians (although the
love commandment does not appear); and, unlike the author of
Colossians, who made of love a crowning virtue, the author of
Ephesians understands that it is more true to the Pauline tradition
for *agapē* to be that principle upon which ethical particulars may
be based. Thus Ephesians refers to the Christian as "rooted and
fixed in love" (3:17). It is true that the immediate further point
that the author makes here relates *agapē* to the esoteric knowledge
in which he is so interested (cf. vv. 18 f.), but he shortly, in the
paraenetic section of the letter (chaps. 4–6), returns to *agapē* as
the fundamental underlying ethical principle. Right at the first of
this paraenetic section (4:2), the author refers in general terms to

6. Cf. the discussion of this point by Francis W. Beare, "The Epistle to the Colossians: Introduction and Exegesis," in *The Interpreter's Bible*, vol. 11, p. 211.
7. On this point, see again Kümmel, *Introduction to the New Testament*, pp.
251–56.

Christians who are "bearing one another in love," and in 5:2 he uses the general Pauline expression, "walk in love." Here he adds further, "just as Christ also loved us," a reference to the exemplary role of Christ's self-sacrifice on the cross (5:2), and in 4:15 he refers to "speaking the truth in love."

Ephesians is truer to Paul's view than is Colossians when the author considers love to be, not a crowning virtue, but a basic ethical norm, even a general orientation ("walking"). Paul, of course, viewed *agapē* as the summary of God's commands beyond which nothing really needed to be said (Rom. 13), even as the summary of his whole gospel (1 Cor. 13). When Paul went further to expand on the implications of the love commandment in detail, as he did, for example, in 1 Cor. 8 and Rom. 14, that was hardly an attempt to set up generally valid ethical regulations, as the authors of Colossians and Ephesians now do, but rather an attempt to make love relevant to a particular situation in view of the coming eschaton. For Ephesians, furthermore, as for Colossians, *agapē* is really only formally present, as one sees when the author refers to "bearing one another in love" in 4:2 and to "speaking the truth in love" in 4:15. Apparently, for the author of Ephesians, bearing one another and speaking the truth are made specifically Christian by the addition of the words, "in love."

Ephesians is also similar to Colossians in its eschatology, which of course goes hand in hand with the above observations about *agapē*. Here the eschatology is even more notable by its absence than in Colossians, since there is virtually no eschatology in Ephesians. The closest the author comes to a true eschatological statement is 5:16, "redeeming the time," which he has taken from Col. 4:5. Already in Colossians, however, this eschatologically loaded phrase has ceased to refer to the coming end time, but rather to the need to use present time—dare we say it?—more efficiently. The complete statement in Colossians reads, "Walk in wisdom regarding those outside, redeeming the time"—that is to say, the most efficient way to deal with non-Christians is sagaciously. Tell them what they want to hear (v. 6, "Know how you ought to answer each one"), so that they will not interfere with one's time. In this way one redeems the time; the sentiment approaches Taoism. Ephesians actually returns the phrase, "re-

deeming the time," somewhat to its eschatological orientation by
adding the words, "for the days are evil" (Eph. 5:16). The author
lets the matter drop there, however, and does not actually go
further to draw the conclusion that, because the days are evil,
God is soon to come with his righteous judgment. Rather, like
the author of Colossians, he explains how to get along in evil
days, i.e., how to redeem the time (don't get drunk, sing hymns,
vv. 18–20).

It is in this context that the author of Ephesians comes closest
to the Pauline imperative in the indicative, for in 5:8 he writes,
"You were then darkness, but now light in the Lord. Walk as
children of light!"[8] We have here, then, exactly the same understanding as in Colossians; because the Christian has already been
saved, he must now bring his earthly existence into line with the
model of that saved existence. This is the function of the "just as
Christ loved us" in 5:2—or 5:1, "Become imitators of God";
Christ's love is understood as the model of saved existence. In this
respect, there is even less of an inner consistency between imperative and indicative than in Colossians, for the concept of the hid-
denness of one's having been saved, explicitly mentioned in
Colossians, drops out in Ephesians. Perhaps that concept glimmers through in Eph. 2:7 where, after affirming in the strongest
way possible that the Christian has already been resurrected, the
author gives as God's motive for that salvation "that he may point
out in the aeons yet to come the exceeding wealth of his grace."
Whether this means what the author of Colossians meant by his
affirmation that the Christian's life "has been hidden with Christ
in God" is, however, unclear. The author of Ephesians may be
referring to the continuing presence of Christian existence in a
hostile world.

Exactly as in Colossians, one finds in Ephesians an interest in
defining the Christian, over against the non-Christian, by reference
to ethics. This interest is much more pronounced in Ephesians,
however, so that the author writes, "Remember that then you
were gentiles in flesh, . . . for you were at that time apart from
Christ, . . . foreigners to the covenants of the promise, having no
hope, and without God in the world" (Eph. 2:11 f.). That old,

8. Cf. also 4:1, which is discussed below.

hopeless existence is, however, set over against the new creation "in Christ Jesus for good works" (v. 10)..

The problem of the inner consistency of imperative and indicative for both Colossians and Ephesians is that the Pauline eschatological reservation on the indicative side has been removed in favor of the concept of a saved society. If I am already saved, however, if I have already been, as Eph. 2:5 f. affirms, "made alive together with Christ . . . raised together and seated together with him in the high heavenly places," why, indeed, ought I to behave? Why does the problem even arise? Colossians and Ephesians answer the former question in the same way. First, I must understand myself as having an existence in two places at once, heaven and earth, and must strive to bring my earthly existence into line with my heavenly existence. Why I must do that is developed in neither Colossians nor Ephesians; that I must do so is inherited Pauline deposit. Secondly, to act ethically, to behave as a Christian should, is the way in which I show that Christians are different from others.[9]

Behaving as a Christian should, however, becomes quite problematical when one realizes the large degree to which such behavior is indistinguishable, for Colossians and Ephesians, from popular morality in both Judaism and paganism in the Roman world.[10] The prominence of the *Haustafeln* (rules for conduct in a household) and of the catalogs of vices and virtues in Colossians and Ephesians, frequently discussed in the literature, are the

---

9. That this is a marked tendency of these and the later Epistles of the Pauline corpus is especially well seen by A. F. J. Klijn, "Die Ethik des Neuen Testaments. Eine Umschau," *Nederlands Theologisch Tijdscrift* 24 (1970): 246. This tendency of course has a positive side, which is to influence non-Christians favorably. Klijn makes this point especially well, as does also Peter Lippert, *Leben als Zeugnis*.

10. That the particulars of the *Haustafeln* and of the catalogs of vices and virtues (see below) are probably Hellenistic Jewish (originally Stoic) material uncritically taken over by Christianity and not anything originally or uniquely Christian (alluded to already above, p. 65) is a point that is not to be debated here. The reader is referred to the discussions of Karl Weidinger, *Die Haustafeln*, pp. 10–50; of Preisker, *Das Ethos des Urchristentums*, pp. 33–36; of Martin Dibelius, *An die Kolosser Epheser an Philemon*, pp. 49 f.; of Hans Lietzmann, *An die Römer*, HNT (Tübingen, 1933), p. 351; and of B. S. Easton, "New Testament Ethical Lists," *JBL* 51 (1932): 1–12. To this I must add that the article by Wolfgang Schrage, "Zur Ethik der neutestamentlichen Haustafeln," *NTS* 21 (1974): 1–22—which appeared after the present work had gone to press—has convinced me at last that there were thoroughgoing conscious attempts by the several New Testament writers to Christianize the *Haustafeln*. This awareness does not, however, alter the remarks made immediately below.

primary case in point. Beare has accurately described the role of
the *Haustafeln* in these letters in his reference to Col. 3:18–4:1:
"We cannot fail to be struck by the meagerness of the instruction
given to the different family groups, and by the entire lack of
appeal to any specifically Christian motive in the exhortations to
husbands and to fathers, and the indefiniteness and generality of
the Christian motivation adduced in the address to wives and to
children."[11] Of course, these *Haustafeln*[12] appear in Christian
form, but the Christianity is not definitive. It may be, as Lohse
thinks, that the advice to slaves in Col. 3:22 grows out of Christian
reflection on the problem of Christian freedom as regards slaves,[13]
but it seems more likely that 3:22 is simply a further example of
the way in which this visible life is to be brought into harmony
with the invisible one. Thus the author advises obedience to
"masters" (literally "lords") on the paradigm of obedience to the
Lord. Aside from this, one may agree with Dibelius that the
Colossians *Haustafel* has "scant originally Christian material."[14]
Beare accurately analyses the motivation of Col. 3:22 when he
observes, "The fading of the eschatological expectation weakened
the force of the appeal to endure a situation [sc. slavery] which
was in any case fleeting. . . . The new motive was found in the
acceptance of the lowly status of the slave as the sphere of service
appointed for one by Christ."[15]

The author of Ephesians has clearly sought to make of the
Haustafel in Colossians something distinctively Christian,[16] especially in 5:25–33, where he discusses proper connubial relationships. We must be clear, however, that what is advised here is not
a new standard of conduct derived from Christian theology but

11. Beare, *Interpreter's Bible*, vol. 11, p. 226.
12. The *Haustafel* in Ephesians appears at Eph. 5:22–6:9 and is an expansion of
the *Haustafel* in Colossians.
13. Lohse, *Colossians and Philemon*, pp. 159 f.
14. Dibelius, *An die Kolosser*, p. 49.
15. Beare, *Interpreter's Bible*, vol. 11, p. 227.
16. So also Lohse, *Colossians and Philemon*, p. 156, n. 13; Dibelius, *An die Kolosser*, p. 49. Lohse evaluates this attempt theologically positively: "Man's relationships
with his fellow man are the field upon which the Christian proves his obedience to
the Lord insofar as he conducts his life in 'love' (*agapē*)" (pp. 156 f.). Valid as this
position may be theologically, it of course nevertheless confirms what has been
brought out here repeatedly—that is, that Colossians and Ephesians are not really
providing ethical guidelines.

rather a familiar standard of conduct that is now given a new base. Again it is Lohse who has summed up the matter succinctly. He writes, "A distinction must be drawn between the ethical directives which were developed in the cultural environment and their adoption and new justification by the Christian community."[17]

The *Haustafeln* must therefore be seen as completely worthless for Christian ethics. Coming early into the post-Pauline tradition,[18] they do not even serve a useful function for the authors of Colossians and Ephesians; for the *Haustafeln* cannot truly be guides (in spite of the attempt in Col. 3:22) for helping to bring this life into harmony with the life beyond unless the life beyond is really no different from the non-Christian world—something that both authors would hotly deny.[19] The *Haustafeln*, by the same token, do not mark off Christian existence from non-Christian existence, since the regulations are by and large derived from non-Christian sources. In Eduard Lohse's words, "In the ethics of Hellenistic popular philosophy, which was probably transmitted to the Christian communities via the Hellenistic synagogues, there was a rich collection of material from which a person could ascertain what was generally considered proper conduct."[20]

The pitfall into which the authors of Colossians and Ephesians have fallen is the attempt to hold on to the assumption, derived from Paul, that a Christian needs to be advised to be ethically somehow different from everyone else and at the same time to affirm that the Christian has been saved. When, in the tradition of Paul, the distinctive mark of the Pauline Christian—his faith—

17. Lohse, *Colossians and Philemon*, p. 155, n. 4. Cf. also Preisker, *Das Ethos des Urchristentums*, p. 213.

18. Paul himself never dabbled with such insignificant popular morality; a *Haustafel* appears in the post-Pauline letters, aside from Col. 3:18–4:1 and Eph. 5:21–6:9, only at 1 Pet. 2:13–3:7. Similar lists in Titus 2:1–10, 1 Tim. 2:8–12, and 6:1–2 will be discussed below.

19. This statement will surely come as a shock to a former colleague, who once observed that Ephesians must surely have been written by Paul, because Eph. 5:25 told him how to love his wife! Precisely the problem of using the *Haustafeln* as "forms in which what was fulfilled could be presented and made useful" was early recognized by Karl Weidinger in his ground breaking work, *Die Haustafeln*, p. 8. Cf. further the judgment of Easton, "Ethical Lists," p. 12, that "the danger in the New Testament period lay in appropriating current Stoic formulas as satisfactory ends in themselves." This appropriation is viewed positively by Heinz-Dietrich Wendland, *Ethik des Neuen Testaments*, pp. 68 f., who thinks that Christians in this way avoided being "on the borders of the world."

20. Lohse, *Colossians and Philemon*, p. 156.

disappears from sight, the most obvious distinguishing mark left
to which later Paulinists could turn was ethics; but the attempt to
hold this ethical definition of the Christian in some kind of unity
with Paul's eschatology fails, because it loosens the dialectical
position of the Christian who lives in faith from the eschatological
hope that is formally retained,[21] allows it to drift into antiquity,
and replaces it with a concept of salvation already—a concept that
is logically inconsistent with ethical demands, which must now
be sought, not within the implications of Pauline theology, but
in the environment.

The same remarks are valid regarding the same authors' use of
catalogs of vices and virtues. Paul had certainly used such catalogs,
and in somewhat the same way (cf. 1 Cor. 6:9–11; Gal. 5:16–25);[22]
he certainly expected the man of faith to walk ethically.[23] For
Paul, however, there was valid reason: life in faith was a precarious position! The Christian was in danger of allowing Flesh to
gain control (Gal. 5:13, "Do not allow freedom to become an
occasion for the flesh")[24] and thus should live righteously, in
keeping with his having been declared righteous. Yet just when
he advanced such a position, Paul added the command to love,
Gal. 5:14, which he clearly understood to be eschatological demand. (Cf. the discussion of Rom. 13 above in chap. 3.)[25] When,

21. Victor Paul Furnish, *The Love Command in the New Testament*, p. 122, also
emphasizes the absence of the Pauline dialectic in Colossians and Ephesians.
22. Rom. 1:29–31, often cited as an example (cf. Siegfried Wibbing, *Die Tugend-
und Lasterkataloge im Neuen Testament und ihre Traditiongeschichte unter besonderer Berücksichtigung der Qumran-Texte*), ought really not to be counted here,
since it belongs to the straw man gentile whom Paul sets up in order to prove that
all men are sinners. Rom. 3:10–20.
23. Wibbing, *Tugend- und Lasterkataloge*, p. 124, makes this point especially well.
24. Cf. also ibid., p. 110.
25. One will have to confess that, in 1 Cor. 6:9–11, Paul's use of a catalog of vices
was the same as the use of such catalogs in Colossians and Ephesians to the degree
that he cited a list of generally recognized vices, not derived, by antithesis, from
faith or love and not a direct command of the Spirit and by the list intended to
mark off non-Christian existence from Christian existence. Yet, even here, the underlying rationale is not that the Christian should make his earthly life like his
already attained heavenly life, but rather that he should live out his justification
("You were justified," v. 11). Paul was, furthermore, probably led to use such a list
in this way because of the libertinistic situation that had developed in Corinth,
which he in fact viewed as a false interpretation of Christian freedom. One may in
fact understand the ethical position of Colossians and Ephesians as a further misunderstanding growing out of Paul's refutation of Corinthian libertinism. The belief that salvation has occurred is retained, but libertinism is rejected in favor of
an ethics like Paul's.

then, one finds in Col. 3:5–13 and in Eph. 4:17–5:5 lists of vices and virtues, one will have to recognize that these have the same function as the *Haustafeln* and do not function in a truly Pauline way. The lists seek to bring earthly existence into line with heavenly existence (Col. 3:5, "Put to death, therefore, the members that are on earth") or to set off the Christian from the non-Christian (Eph. 4:17, "Walk no longer as the gentiles walk").[26] The Pauline eschatology and love principle are then only secondarily (after reinterpretation) brought in as further support for the paraenesis.

Wibbing has observed that

> . . . concrete relationships in the individual congregations did not determine the enumeration of concepts in any of the catalogs of virtues. One can, however, correctly assume that the general theme of a letter, such as, in Ephesians, the unity of the church made up of Jews and pagans, . . . caused the appearance of one or another virtue in a catalog.[27]

In thus remarking, Wibbing has brought to attention what in fact stands out in Ephesians—that is, that the true ethical goal is the unity of the church. Unity is certainly an authentic Pauline concept. In 1 Cor. 1–3 Paul argued extensively for the unity of the Corinthian church, and in Phil. 1:27 he made a strong appeal for unity in the face of affliction. For Paul, of course, unity in the church was an implication of the unity of eschatological reality. Phil. 1:27 urges unity in one spirit, unity in maintaining faith; and in 1 Corinthians it is a matter of one lord of the congregation —not Paul and Apollos and Peter, but Christ. In Ephesians, however, unity is blown up to be the supreme theological and ethical reality. The word *henotēs*, unity, appears in the New Testament only in Eph. 4:3, where the writer appeals to the readers to keep the "unity of the spirit," and in 4:13,where he hopes for a "unity of faith and of knowledge." (Phil. 1:27 may glimmer in the background here.) By unity, however, the author of Ephesians has two things in mind, which he equates. One is the mythical concept of the divine Man who reunites the disunited All into himself; the other is the unity of the church that brings together

26. Cf. Wibbing, *Tugend- und Lasterkataloge*, p. 123, "for the most part abstract concepts."
27. Ibid., p. 100.

Jewish and gentile congregations.[28] It has been elsewhere abundantly demonstrated that this central theological point in Ephesians is developed by the author's demythologizing the mythical Man into the church, the body of Christ, which is where the unity is now seen to exist, if only as a goal.[29]

Here, then, at last, theology and ethics come together in a thoroughly consistent way in Ephesians, for the unity that is affirmed to have happened in the theological section of the letter (chaps. 1–3) is then the most important challenge of the paraenetic section (chaps. 4–6). Most strongly does the author affirm the unity in 2:5 f.: "made alive *together* with Christ . . . and raised *together* and seated *together* with him in the high heavenly places in Christ Jesus." This unity then becomes the ethical goal discussed at length at the opening of the paraenetic section, 4:1–16. Here it is hoped that "we, the All, may grow up into him who is the head" (4:15), and it is thus regarding the unity that a true imperative in the indicative appears in Ephesians. "Walk worthy of the calling to which you were called," urges Eph. 4:1, and the author then launches immediately into his appeal for unity. The author of Ephesians apparently also understands the entirety of the paraenetic section—the *Haustafeln*, the catalog of vices and virtues, and the other admonitions found there—to be implied by the indicative of salvation stated at the first of chapter 2, although here it is not a matter of imperative *in* indicative; rather, his point is that salvation implies the need for right ethical behavior. "We are what he has wrought," affirms Eph. 2:10, "created in Christ Jesus for good works!" (Paul is turning over in his grave.) Given this description of salvation, it then naturally follows that the paraenetic section, after enjoining unity, proceeds to call for various good works. The only problem, as has been discussed above, is that there is now no rationale for the choice of certain

28. Paul, in spite of his loyalty to Jerusalem, was of course to a great degree himself responsible for the split between Jewish and gentile Christianity.

29. Cf. Heinrich Schlier, *Christus und die Kirche im Epheserbrief*, Beiträge zur historischen Theologie, 6 (Tübingen, 1930), pp. 27–37; idem, "Die Kirche nach dem Brief an die Epheser," in *Die Kirche im Epheserbrief*, by Heinrich Schlier and Viktor Warnach (Münster/Westfallen, 1949), p. 84; idem, *Der Brief an die Epheser* (Düsseldorf, 1962), pp. 121–33; and my own work, *The New Testament Christological Hymns*, Society for New Testament Studies Monograph Series, 15 (Cambridge, 1971), pp. 88–92.

good works, especially when they turn out to be no different from the good works that Stoics or Hellenistic Jews or others would have selected.

Whereas the main theme of Ephesians is the unity of the church, a theme that has both its theological and its ethical side, the main theme of Colossians is the opposition of "heresy" (2:8–23). Thus, there is in Colossians no inner coherence between theology and ethics as it appears in Ephesians; nevertheless, the theme of unity in the church does appear in the paraenetic section of Colossians. In Col. 3:10 f. the readers are enjoined to "put on the new man, renewed in knowledge according to the image of his creator, where there is not Greek and Jew, circumcision and uncircumcision, barbarian and Scythian, slave and free man, but Christ is all and in all." "Put on" is then repeated at the beginning of verse 12, after which comes the list of virtues that culminates in *agapē* (v. 14). Thus, the unity of all groups in the church is, at the first of the paraenetic section in Colossians, linked with the ethical exhortations. One may in fact say that the unity of diverse groups in the church, which is the main theme of Ephesians, and explicitly so, is by implication equally as important in Colossians; for the problem of the "heresy" in chapter 2 is that the unity of faith (cf. Eph. 4:13) is endangered. This is seen right away in Colossians when the author affirms that the readers have been reconciled if they "abide in the faith fixed and steadfast, and do not shift from the hope of the gospel which [they] heard" (Col. 1:23). In Colossians, therefore, as in Ephesians, unity stands on both the theological and the ethical side, albeit in a considerably less emphatic way than in Ephesians. It is true of both Epistles that unity in the church is in reality the most fundamental ethical injunction, the one which coheres completely with the theological positions of the two letters, and the one which is understood as in some—by no means altogether thought out—way implying the individual ethical admonitions.

Boiled down, then, the ethical position of Colossians and Ephesians may be summarized as an appeal for unity in the church, which is made up of Christians who ought to make their visible, present existence like their invisible, heavenly existence and thereby show that Christians are ethically different from others.

As we have seen, the ethical particulars are, upon scrutiny, reduced to zero. The attempt to make Christians different from
others and like heavenly citizens is in reality an attempt to make
Christians simply good people. The attempt is self-defeating. One
could hardly argue that the modern Christian—or modern man in
general—has anything to learn from this position, unless one would
be willing to drop the contention that Christianity is in some way
unique. The grounding that Colossians and Ephesians give, of
course, to the attempt to make Christians into good people is a
Christian grounding, a Christian foundation; and perhaps one
would be content to let Christian existence equal whatever is
generally accepted as being good. There can be no doubt that
most Christians today in fact make just that equation! But then
Christianity is reduced to a cipher; it is indistinguishable from
the world, and we can learn nothing from Colossians and Ephesians relevant to our ethical situation today. The loss of the
Pauline expectation of the Parousia has solved the Pauline ethical
problem only by dissolving it.

There remains only the unity of the church. Colossians and
Ephesians, inheriting this principle from Paul, make it, in two
steps, into a dominant ethical position. Here one may perhaps
better observe than suggest. Such a position is surely a catholic
position, and the ecumenical forces recently at work have in fact
drawn considerable attention especially to Ephesians. The degree
to which the ecumenical movement, however, is motivated by a
desire to make earthly existence conform to heavenly existence is
open to question. A variety of political, sociological, economic,
and intellectual, as well as theological factors brought about the
Protestant Reformation (as also earlier and later schisms), and the
same variety of causes appears to be bringing certain groups together today. Certainly as Christian churches lose membership in
staggering proportions all over the world, as the cost of maintaining large, bureaucratic institutions becomes impractical, as the
"world come of age" replaces Christendom, Christian groups will
tend to unite (or reunite). Whether that is "good" or "bad" can,
however, be decided—aside from utilitarian criteria relevant only
to the existence of the church as an institution—only when one
discovers where the ecumenical movement is leading ethically.

But by that statement we imply that the principle of the unity of the church is to be judged, ethically speaking, by an outside criterion. The principle of unity itself does not give ethical guidance to man and his world today.

2 THESSALONIANS, PASTORAL EPISTLES, 1 PETER

These early Christian tracts in the Pauline tradition may be considered together, not so much because they are later (in the case of 2 Thessalonians, at least, the time of writing may be no later than Ephesians, if as late), but because they represent a second stage of development—some would call it corruption—after Colossians and Ephesians, away from the distinctive elements of Pauline theology and ethics toward fixed ecclesiastical tradition.

Of these writings, only 1 Peter makes love in any way central. "Love one another from your hearts persistently," urges 1 Pet. 1:22, and, similarly, 4:8 calls the readers "before everything, [to] hold on persistently to your love for yourselves (i.e., one another)." In 1 Tim. 1:5 it is asserted that "the goal (*telos*) of the proclamation is *agapē*"; but the author shows immediately that he understands love to be subject to qualification by other criteria when he adds, "from a pure heart and a good conscience and a faith that is not hypocritical." It is clear, furthermore, that this love is only formally present in 1 Timothy, since it does not elsewhere appear in the Epistle, except to turn up as *one* virtue among others in 6:11: "Pursue righteousness, piety, faith, love, endurance, gentleness of temper."[30] What seems to be essentially the same list, although with variations in each case, appears again at 2 Tim. 2:22 as well as at 2 Tim. 3:10. The contrast to Col. 3:12–14 should be apparent; *agapē* was there the crowning virtue, here only one virtue among others.[31] *Agapē* as designation of Christian behavior does not occur in 2 Thessalonians or in Titus.

The eschatology of these letters is, with few exceptions, notable by its absence, as was the case with Ephesians. The most prominent exception is, of course, the well-known discussion of the last

30. Cf. also Preisker, *Das Ethos des Urchristentums*, p. 201. C. Spicq, *Saint Paul: Les Épîtres pastorales*, vol. 1, p. 286, calls attention to the fact that "believers" and "beloved" are almost synonymous in 1 Tim. 6:2.

31. So also Furnish, *The Love Command*, pp. 127 f.

day in 2 Thess. 2:1–12. This passage in no way, however, presents the imminent eschatology familiar to us from Paul's letters; rather, it is a rejection of imminence. "Unless the apostasy first come and the Lawless Man be revealed, the Son of Perdition," the author counsels in 2:3, one should not be concerned about the eschaton. Since these things obviously have not occurred and are not occurring—such seems to be the drift of the passage—the end is not soon. Furthermore, the highly formalized stylized picture of the end time presented in 2 Thess. 2:1–12 is more like the Apocalypse than like Paul. In any case, the passage stands singularly apart from the rest of the letter and is unrelated to anything else in 2 Thessalonians, including ethics. Only 1 Peter still connects eschatology to ethics and precisely to the ethical principle of love.[32] To be sure, no implications are drawn from this connection, Christianity is not described as eschatological existence, and the ethical directions which fill much of 1 Peter are unrelated to *agapē*; nevertheless, the formal connection, inherited from Paul, between imminence and the imperative to love does still find expression in 4:7 f.: "The end of all things has drawn near, therefore be sensible and sober for your prayers, and before everything hold on persistently to your love for one another."[33]

1 Peter also continues the Pauline tradition of the imperative in the indicative (the other letters here being considered do not), although with the modification made by Colossians and Ephesians —that is, that the indicative no longer has the Pauline eschatological reservation about it but is rather an indicative of salvation already. Thus one reads in 1 Pet. 2:10 f., "You are those who were then 'not a people' but now 'a people of God,' 'who had not received mercy but now have received mercy.' Beloved, I call upon you . . . to keep away from the fleshly passions." The *form* of the

---

32. So also J. N. D. Kelly, *A Commentary on the Epistles of Peter and Jude*, p. 177.

33. C. H. Dodd, *Gospel and Law* (New York, 1951), p. 29, understands this passage to give evidence of the passing of Paul's "overwrought mood of expectation" and its being replaced by the view that "this whole order of civilization, this whole historical process as we have known it, has no necessary permanence." I do not find that kind of demythologized eschatology in 1 Peter, least of all in this passage. Rather, the eschatology is generally replaced (although the language is retained, especially in this passage), as in Colossians and Ephesians, by the view that this present existence is unreal, and that the real existence is yet to be attained, although in a sense it has been attained already. 1 Peter's terms are "perishable/imperishable" (1:23 and elsewhere).

imperative in the indicative, the indicative again referring to what has been completed, is also found in 1 Pet. 1:22, where the indicative, however, refers not to God's gracious act of salvation but to the readers' having accomplished self-purification: "Having purified your lives [as just explained in 1:13–21] in the obedience of truth leading to brotherly love (*philadelphia*), love one another from your hearts persistently."

Like Colossians and Ephesians, 1 Peter also encourages the readers to show by their behavior that they are different from non-Christians—again an emphasis that is not present in the pastoral Epistles and 2 Thessalonians. Thus we find in 1 Pet. 4:3, "The time that is past was sufficient for doing what the gentiles wish"; then follows a catalog of vices. This appears in 1 Peter, however, without the note that was so prominent in Colossians and Ephesians, that the Christian by so doing was at the same time bringing his earthly life into harmony with his already attained heavenly existence; although 1 Peter does, as has been seen, also keep the view that salvation has already been attained. Thus, that the Christian is commanded to be what he already in fact is, and that he is urged to make himself different from others are elements from Colossians and Ephesians that appear in 1 Peter, but without being brought into any consistent position or even into connection with each other.

Aside from 2 Thessalonians, all the Epistles in this group are by and large ethical tracts. They are filled with *Haustafeln*, lists of vices and virtues, and other sundry ethical injunctions.[34] The long *Haustafel* in 1 Pet. 2:13–3:7 is particularly interesting, since the author has consistently employed here the principle of the *imitatio Christi*, suffering as Christ suffered. The principle is expressly stated in 2:21, "Christ suffered for your sakes, leaving behind an example for you";[35] and he then lays emphasis on the submission side of the *Haustafel*—that is, that slaves should be

34. Preisker, *Das Ethos des Urchristentums*, pp. 197, 199, 209, regards this aspect as the result of the influence on Christianity of "Jewish moralism."
35. It is particularly interesting to see what has happened to Pauline theology here. The Pauline *hyper hymōn* (for your sakes), which meant for Paul that Christ died to reveal God's righteousness and to testify to justification through faith (Rom. 3:21–6) or to reveal God's love, which is the same thing (Rom. 5:6–8), has now come to mean that Christ died as an example of proper behavior. Thus, precisely where the same language is kept, salvation through faith is turned into salvation through works.

submissive to masters and wives to husbands.[36] One gets the distinct impression that it is easier to be a Christian if one is either a slave or a woman, although everyone is certainly given his chance in the opening admonition to "be subject to every human authority for the sake of the Lord"; king and governors are then specifically mentioned (1 Pet. 2:13 f.).[37] Dibelius has referred to this dominant theme of the *Haustafel* in 1 Peter as showing "a particular and valuable manner of Christianizing,"[38] and Selwyn has also sought to evaluate the passage positively. As he puts the matter: "It seems as though St. Peter found in the lives of those whose functions were, in one way or another, subordinate, the best expression of, and the best opportunities for expressing, the Christian way of life."[39] Kelly, further, excuses the author by explaining that Christians "had entered into a relationship of brotherhood with one another in which ordinary social distinctions, real enough in the daily round of life in the world, had lost all meaning."[40]

Surely this manner of approving the *Haustafel* in 1 Peter must be rejected as naïve, even base. One must see clearly what a truly horrible thing has occurred here, within the development of Pauline traditions, to the Pauline ethical norm of concern for

36. It has not infrequently been suggested that this portion of 1 Peter may rely in part on Rom. 13. One may note, for example, the presence in both Rom. 13:1 and 1 Pet. 2:13 of the words *hypotassō* (to subject [oneself]) and *hyperechō* (to be superior—applied to rulers). Weidinger, *Die Haustafeln*, p. 63, thinks of only a common background.

37. In 2:17 the commands to "love the brotherhood" and to "fear God" occur side by side. Furnish, *The Love Command*, p. 164, lifts these two imperatives out of the list and argues that they "form a distinctive but recognizable version of the double commandment of the Synoptic tradition." Given that the fear of God is in Deuteronomy virtually synonymous with the love of God (Deuteronomy being of course the ultimate origin of this commandment), it may be that the tradition of the double command to love has influenced the close connection of these two imperatives in 1 Pet. 2:17, but hardly more than that. It is not even immediately obvious that the juxtaposition of these two imperatives is anything more than coincidence. Thus Wilhelm Brandt, "Wandel als Zeugnis nach dem 1. Petrusbrief," in *Verbum Dei manet in aeternum. Festschrift Otto Schmitz* (Witten, 1953), p. 18 takes "honor all, love the brotherhood" together, and then "fear God, honor the king." Such a division does justice to the parallelism in the verse. Submission is in any case the overriding theme here, and 2:17 is to be read as further examples of submission. Furnish, *The Love Command*, pp. 165 f., approaches such an interpretation himself.

38. Dibelius, *An die Kolosser*, p. 49.

39. Edward Gordon Selwyn, *The First Epistle of St. Peter*, p. 91, cf. further pp. 101 f. Selwyn actually wrongs the author of 1 Peter to the degree that the author, in this passage, tries to explicate a situation in which all Christians could be submissive, as 2:13 f. shows.

40. Kelly, *Peter and Jude*, p. 115. Kelly and the author of 1 Peter seem to me to be discussing two different things.

one's fellow man. Paul endorsed the complete going out of one-self for the sake of the other that is involved in *agapē*; thus, he knew that *agapē* was a way of living not in this world, but in the next, and he knew that the Christian who loves goes out of the world by going out of himself for the welfare of his fellow man. This may certainly be understood as submission, as self-sacrifice—but for the other. Once the *Haustafeln*, however, came into the Pauline tradition, it was probably inevitable that someone would "Christianize" one, as the author of 1 Peter did. But to Chris-tianize by institutionalizing! Could the author not have applied *agapē* in the Pauline sense to the *Haustafel*, thus bringing the *Haustafel* up to a consistent concept of submission, whereby *every* human situation would have been seen as an opportunity to love, to respond to the needs of one's fellow human beings? Instead of this, however, our author in effect endorses a society that supports submission institutionally; or, as Weidinger puts it, "The rule about slaves in this *Haustafel* has the deepest motivation that we encounter in early Christianity for the demand to persevere in slavery."[41] All interest in one's fellow man is out, concern with living up to a standard of personal submission *for one's own sake* is in. It is very probably true, as Selwyn has observed, "that these relationships provided the sociological framework within which Christians . . . had to live";[42] but the observation is almost trite. Stated otherwise, we see that the *Haustafel* in 1 Peter does exactly what the *Haustafeln* in Colossians and Ephesians do; it simply has the effect of making Christianity indistinguishable from the world around it, the opposite of what the author really intended.

The first regulation of the *Haustafel* in 1 Peter, that Christians should be submissive to king and governors, has the effect of mak-ing Christians into good citizens.[43] (The same things happen in 2 Thess. 3:6–12, only there it is *working* citizens.)[44] This is also true of lists of ethical injunctions in the pastoral Epistles that re-

---

41. Weidinger, *Die Haustafeln*, p. 64.

42. Selwyn, *First Epistle of St. Peter*, p. 104.

43. Spicq, *Saint Paul*, vol. 1, p. 291, observes that in the pastoral Epistles one is to take on "the obligations proper to his age, to his sex, and to his condition"; cf. further pp. 293–95.

44. This passage is not, as is often thought, related to the eschatological discussion of 2 Thess. 2:1–12. That stands by itself and is unrelated to the rest of the Epistle.

semble *Haustafeln* (1 Tim. 2:8–12; 6:1–2; Titus 2:1–10), although
with an interesting twist. The clue to the somewhat altered viewpoint is given in 1 Tim. 3:15, "That you may know how it is
necessary to behave in the household of God, which is the church."
Thus, in the pastoral Epistles, ethics now becomes the equivalent
of church order, which, to be sure, is not narrowly viewed simply
as ecclesiastical polity but is seen as the whole order of living that
is proper within the church.[45] The church has now become that
ship sailing through hostile seas,[46] and those who wish not to
drown come aboard; but that means all the way aboard. This
viewpoint may also be seen in the different view that the pastoral
Epistles take toward the Christian's relationship with non-Christians from the view taken by 1 Peter (also Colossians and Ephesians). 1 Peter, as was seen, continues to want Christians to
distance themselves from the conduct of "gentiles"; the pastoral
Epistles, however, seem to urge non-contact with non-Christians.
Thus the pastoral Epistles frequently admonish the avoidance of
theological discussion or conflict (1 Tim. 6:20; 2 Tim. 2:16, 23;
Titus 1:10 f.; 3:9). Although these references apparently refer to
theological conflict within Christianity, one may perhaps assume
that they take for granted that one should shun theological discussion outside the church as well—except for the purpose of
converting persons to Christianity. In keeping with this position,
the "be submissive to king and governor" of 1 Pet. 2:13 f. becomes
in 1 Tim. 2:1–4 an injunction to pray for such men, in order that
they may be converted to Christianity!

In the *Haustafel*-like passages in the pastoral Epistles, then, the
regulations are for life in the church.[47] 1 Tim. 2:8–12 explains

45. This point is made excellently by Martin Dibelius, *The Pastoral Epistles*, 3d
ed. rev., trans. Philip Buttolph and Adela Yarbro, Hermeneia (Philadelphia, 1972),
pp. 39–41. It seems to have been unavoidable that Christianity would move in this
direction as the imminent expectation was dropped. Preisker, *Das Ethos des Urchristentums*, p. 217, states: "the longer the congregations are in the world, the more
middle-class they become, and the more they must concern themselves with the
securing of their existence in the world, to this degree office and external regulation become more important." A similar statement is made by Franz Joseph
Schierse, "Eschatologische Existenz und christliche Bürgerlichkeit," *Geist und
Leben* 32 (1959): 280.

46. Note the "suffered shipwreck" of 1 Tim. 1:19.

47. Here, even more than in 1 Peter, slavery comes in for discussion, although
without the theological grounding given the institution in 1 Peter. Rather, 1 Tim.
6:1 f. and Titus 2:9 f. urge slaves to be good slaves so as not to give Christianity a
black eye! On this point cf. especially Lippert, *Leben als Zeugnis*, p. 52.

how men and women are to perform their functions in the church; and in Titus 2:1–10 the reference to "teachers" (v. 3) and the division into old men/old women, young women/young men shows the ecclesiastical orientation of the regulations. Yet in this passage in Titus the difference between Christianity and good citizenship has altogether disappeared. Furthermore, 1 Timothy is by and large a book of church order, with rules for bishops and deacons in chapter 3 and general regulations for the church in 4:6–6:2 (4:6: "By advising the brethren of these things you will be a good deacon"; 6:2: "Teach and urge these things"), the latter passage including regulations regarding widows and elders.

Finally, a new ethical note is heard in these Epistles, and that is that the Christian is expected to hold fast to the *didachē*, to the apostolic tradition of teaching.[48] "Brethren, stand firm and hold on to the traditions [*paradoseis*] which you were taught [*edidach-thēte*], either by our word or by our epistle" (2 Thess. 2:15). The readers are advised in 2 Tim. 1:13 to "hold the example of sound words which you heard from me," and 3:14 puts it almost exactly as 2 Thessalonians: "abide in those teachings which you learned and on which you relied, knowing from whom you learned them." Further, Titus 1:9 calls for a bishop to "hold firmly on to the reliable doctrine that is in accordance with the teaching [*didachē*], so that he may . . . be able to urge the congregation in sound instruction [*didaskalia*]," and 2:1 repeats this admonition when it commands "Titus" to "speak what befits sound instruction." Thus the term *hygiainousa didaskalia* (sound instruction) seems even to have become a technical term for the author of Titus. The most original and perhaps most surprising way of putting this position, however, appears in 1 Timothy, for 1 Tim. 6:13 f. employs the concept of the *imitatio Christi* in a unique way to underscore the need for the congregation to maintain right faith. *Imitatio fidei Christi* in fact replaces *imitatio Christi* when the author of 1 Timothy advises "Timothy," "before . . . Christ Jesus who bore witness to the *good confession* before Pontius Pilate, to keep the commandment without blemish and blame-

---

48. That this follows from the dropping of the earlier eschatology is argued by Preisker, *Das Ethos des Urchristentums*, p. 198. This new element in Christian ethics is probably the result of Stoic influences; cf. idem, p. 211 and n. 2.

less." The "authenticity of the faith" of 1 Pet. 1:7 and the "firm in the faith" of 1 Pet. 5:9 may also be meant in this way, although that is not certain; the phrases may still bear the original Pauline meaning.

These later Epistles in the Pauline tradition, then, have been seen to carry on the movement, begun by Colossians and Ephesians, away from the Pauline theological-eschatological grounding of ethics toward an unreflected ethics that is indistinguishable from good citizenship. The Christian orientation of this ethics is of course still obvious, since reference is always made back, in some way or other, to Christ or to the Christian tradition; but this orientation is definitive for the character of the ethics only where it provides for an endorsement of certain social institutions —slavery, obedience of wife to husband, submission to governing authorities—that many, including many Christians, would be loathe to endorse today.[49]

Here surface two of the most significant problems for any use of the New Testament for ethics today. One is the problem of the canon within the canon; the other is that each age applies its own criteria to Christian tradition.

The term "canon," of course, means rule, originally ruler (i.e., measuring stick). It is the standard by which something is measured. Applied to the New Testament, it normally means that list of twenty-seven books (considered to have apostolic authority) by which Christianity or Christian faith and life are to be measured. The problem of the "canon within the canon" arises, then, when one rule is found somewhere within those twenty-seven books that is at variance with other portions of the New Testament.[50] Precisely in our study of the development of Christian ethics within the Pauline tradition this problem becomes acute—at least for the person who assumes that the New Testament is in some way

49. Spicq, *Saint Paul*, vol. 1, p. 296, observes the coincidence of Christian and pre-Christian pagan ethics in the pastoral Epistles, but evaluates this positively: "If the Pastorals, just as strongly as the earlier epistles, note the contrast between Christianity and paganism, they do not further isolate the Church from the secular world; to the contrary, they implant in it a remarkable optimism and certainty"; cf. further vol. 2, pp. 633 f.

50. One cannot mention this issue without referring to the excellent discussion by Ernst Käsemann, "The Canon of the New Testament and the Unity of the Church." in *Essays on New Testament Themes*, trans. W. J. Montague, SBT, 41 (Naperville, Ill., 1964), pp. 95–107.

authoritative for ethics today; for now that person is forced to choose. Will he choose Paul? If so, as we saw in chapter 3, he will likely have to take Paul's now impossible eschatology as well. Will he choose the way of the New Testament Paulinists? Here the eschatology is no longer definitive for ethics, but there is the new disadvantage that Christianity now moves in the direction of equating Christian ethics with good citizenship.

At this point, the second problem is interlaced with the first, for it is doubtful that many thinking Christians would be willing to endorse or even to accept the proposition that Christian ethics is nothing more than the best that any society has to offer and that Christians are known by their excelling at generally recognized virtues, not by any kind of distinctive behavior. Actually, there is nothing inherently wrong, viewed from the side of the considera-tion of New Testament ethics, with defining a Christian as just that, as the person who is a paragon of the virtues of a given society. This definition is in fact that which is most often applied in popular piety, as when one employs the statement, "I am not as good a Christian as I should like to be." This statement nor-mally means nothing more nor less than "I am not as good a citizen as I should like to be"; and the traditional equating here in the United States, and in other countries as well (one thinks especially of the "Gott mit uns" of World War I), of national purpose and divine will is merely an expansion, carried to the national level, of the same ethical concept. Thus the person who, for example, opposes American military involvement in the in-ternal affairs of other nations may be accused of opposing Chris-tian values or of being a Communist, which often means the same thing.

The problem with this equation, made in the later Pauline Epistles and still made today, between Christianity and good citizenship is that "time makes ancient good uncouth." Only an extremely small minority of Christians would today endorse hu-man slavery as a valid expression of Christian existence. It is further likely that, within a generation, few will advocate that a Christian woman finds the best expression of her Christianity in submitting to the will of her husband; and there is already a considerable criticism being mounted against the view that good citizenship is the same as being a "good" Christian.

What happens in such a development is obviously that other criteria for ethics are continually brought in and coordinated with Christian tradition. To recognize that is to see at one and the same time that the later Pauline letters do not provide any kind of valid ethics for today and that ethical criteria are perhaps best derived from the context, from one's active involvement in the life, in the society about one, from one's realization, not derived from the New Testament at all, that some things are not right, that some things must be changed.

V

THE JOHANNINE LITERATURE

The Gospel and Epistles of John teach an ethics that is at once almost naïvely simple and yet tantalizing and intriguing. "I give you a new commandment," says the Johannine Jesus, "that you love one another: that you also love one another as I have loved you" (John 13:34); and John 15:12, 17 repeats the commandment exactly: "This is my commandment, that you love one another as I have loved you. . . . I command you these things, that you love one another."[1] This one commandment from the Gospel is then repeated in the Epistles in 1 John 3:11, 23 and 2 John 5.[2]

Apparently, the consistent use of the term, "one another," in place of "neighbor" is a conscious delimiting of the scope of love. Bultmann wishes, as do others,[3] to understand the "one another" not to exclude the "neighbor." Thus he states that "the Christian commandment to love one's neighbor is, of course, neither limited nor annulled by the Johannine commandment to 'love one another.'" The Johannine love *is* intended for the congregation, "but this is no closed group." In other words, "the world constantly has the possibility of being drawn into this circle of mutual

---

1. Cf. Herbert Preisker, *Das Ethos des Urchristentums*, p. 204: "Liebe ist das einzig-eine Gebot, das es überhaupt gibt."

2. Of course, belief is also called for in the Johannine literature; cf. John 14:1 et passim. Especially in chap. 15 do faith and love come together, as is seen in the "abide in me" of v. 4 and the "abide in my love" of v. 9. Cf. the discussion of this point by Rudolf Bultmann, *The Gospel of John*, pp. 539–47, who observes succinctly (p. 547) that "according to John 15 faith and love are, in fact, a unity." Whether love is thereby relieved of its ethical content is a question that we shall have to keep in mind; but believing as ethical commandment does not, in any case, come under our consideration here.

3. Cf. e.g. C. K. Barrett, *The Gospel According to St. John*, p: 377; Josef Kuhl, *Die Sendung Jesu und der Kirche nach dem Johannes-Evangelium*, p. 196; and, apparently, C. H. Dodd, *The Interpretation of the Fourth Gospel*, pp. 404, 423. Cf. also Heinz-Dietrich Wendland, *Ethik des Neuen Testaments*, p. 13. Ambiguous is the statement by André Feuillet, *Johannine Studies*, p. 158.

love."[4] Others, however, have recognized clearly that the Johannine writers do intend for Christian love to be exclusive. As Herbert Preisker put it, "Love has already experienced a narrowing. . . . The depth and warmth of love remain, but it has lost in breadth and unlimitedness."[5] The prominent *Bultmann-Schuler*, Ernst Käsemann, even states flatly that "there is no indication in John that love for one's brother would also include love toward one's neighbor."[6]

Put just in that way, the position of Käsemann will have to be seen as correct. The statement does not exactly disagree with Bultmann's position,[7] only Bultmann wished to emphasize that the circle of loved ones is not closed for John. But is not the mere recognition of a *circle*, only within which it is proper to love, precisely a recognition of the "narrowing," of the "loss in breadth and unlimitedness" (Preisker)? When one recalls that there is abundant evidence that the author of the Fourth Gospel had considerable knowledge of the synoptic tradition and that he consciously altered that tradition at not a few significant points,[8] one will be able only with difficulty to come to any other conclusion than that our author intended a narrowing by *changing* love of neighbor into love of one another.

Käsemann specifically contrasted love of brother to love of neighbor. Although love of *brother* does not occur in the Gospel of John, Käsemann's somewhat inaccurate statement is nevertheless essentially correct, since the term does appear in 1 John, and with the same meaning as "one another" in the Gospel. In 1 John

---

4. Rudolf Bultmann, *Theology of the New Testament*, vol. 2, p. 82. Cf. also idem, *The Gospel of John*, pp. 527–29; and idem, *The Johannine Epistles*, p. 28. Cf. further Kuhl, *Die Sendung Jesu*, p. 104.

5. Preisker, *Das Ethos des Urchristentums*, p. 205. Cf. also R. E. Brown, *The Gospel According to John (xiii-xxi)*, p. 613: "the 'love of one another' of which the Johannine Jesus speaks is love *between Christians*." Brown then defends such love against "the love of all men," which he derides·as "a frequent ideal" of "our own times." Rudolf Schnackenburg, *Die Johannesbriefe*, Herders theologischer Kommentar zum Neuen Testament (Freiburg, Basel, Vienna, 1965³), p. 211, recognizes that the Johannine love is not an expression of "universalism" in contrast to "Jewish particularism," yet (p. 120) he takes the "brothers" of 1 John 3:14 (with Bultmann) to refer as well to others than Christians.

6. Ernst Käsemann, *The Testament of Jesus*, p. 59. So also Hans Conzelmann, *An Outline of the Theology of the New Testament*, pp. 355 f.

7. Above, p. 91.

8. Cf. the evidence marshalled by Barrett, *Gospel According to St. John*, pp. 34–45, and Werner Georg Kümmel, *Introduction to the New Testament*, pp. 142–45.

(cf. 1 John 2:7–11; 3:11–18; 4:16–21), Bultmann is sure that he has a correlation between the Johannine view and that of the synoptic tradition. Regarding these verses in 1 John he writes, " 'Brother' means . . . not especially the Christian comrade in faith, but one's fellow man, the 'neighbor.' "[9] Unfortunately, that simply cannot be the case. 1 John 2:7 f. states: "Beloved, I am not writing a new commandment to you, but an old command- ment which you had from the beginning: the old commandment is the word which you heard. Again, I am writing a new com- mandment to you"; and the author then goes on to refer to the one who loves his brother as being in the light and the one who hates his brother as being in the darkness (vv. 9–11). Can there be any doubt that this "old/new commandment" is the "new commandment" from the Gospel and that the love of brother referred to here is consequently none other than the love of one another commanded in the Gospel? The same will be true for the other two passages in 1 John. In 1 John 3:11 there is a reference to "the announcement which you heard from the beginning" (thus tying this statement to 2:7), "that we love one another." When, then, the discussion shifts in verse 14 to love of brother, one sees that love of brother is synonymous with love of one an- other. When 4:21, finally, brings love of God and love of brother into conjunction, it could be that the synoptic saying about love of God and of neighbor glimmers in the background,[10] but, even if it does, one cannot avoid noticing that precisely the neighbor has been erased and the brother has been written in his place, the brother who can be none other than the brother of 2:7 ff. and 3:11 ff. Certainly the love of one's enemies, known from Matt. 5:44, does not appear in the Johannine literature. Ernst Ḥaenchen has explained the matter exactly. As he analyzes the situation in 1 John, "the conflict situation in which early Christianity stood, not only with Judaism and paganism but also with Christian Gnosticism, narrows the view, so that the Christian now sees only his own congregation."[11]

9. Bultmann, *The Johannine Epistles*, p. 28.

10. Bultmann, *The Johannine Epistles*, p. 76, refers 4:21 back only to 1 John 2:7 ff. and 3:23, not to the synoptic saying.

11. Ernst Haenchen, "Neuere Literatur zu den Johannesbriefen," *ThR* 26 (1960): 37.

The only possibility remaining for viewing the love commandment in the Johannine tradition as intending love outside the
circle of believers is the possibility raised by Bultmann[12] that the
missionary activity of the church originates in love for all men,
i.e., that the "God who so loved the world" of John 3:16 provides
the continuing motivation for the church's ministry. Käsemann
argues that the love of the world appears only here in the Johannine literature, that it may even be only a traditional formulation
employed by the author, and that it by no means gives "us the
right to interpret the whole Johannine proclamation from this
perspective."[13] As a contrast to John 3:16, Käsemann cites 1 John
2:15, "If anyone loves the world, in him is not the love of the
Father";[14] but this is surely a mistaken contrast. God's love of the
world in John 3:16 is his loving concern, his desire to save the
world, as the rest of verse 16 and verse 17 make clear, whereas the
injunction to the church in 1 John 2:15 *not* to love the world
means not to desire the world for oneself, not to wish to be "of
the world." The difference between these two references to loving
the world is the difference between wishing to take the gospel to
all men and wishing to be "worldly," to forsake allegiance to God
for allegiance to "this world."

That the kind of "love of the world" meant in 3:16 is also intended to be carried out by the church, by Christians, is made
clear by the important chapter 17.[15] The author has Jesus say, in
17:18, "Just as thou didst send me into the world, I also have sent
them into the world." That certainly means that the church is to
continue the function of the revealer on earth, and the connection
of this function with the divine love (i.e., of 3:16) is obviously
made when chapter 17 concludes with Jesus explaining that he
has made known God's name to the church "so that the love with
which you loved me may be in them and I in them" (v. 26). Käsemann then correctly concludes that "the disciples' mission in the

12. Above, pp. 91 f. Victor Paul Furnish, *The Love Commandment in the New
Testament*, pp. 143–48, 152–54, also holds that the love command in John includes
even love of enemies.

13. Käsemann, *Testament of Jesus*, pp. 59 f.

14. Ibid., p. 60.

15. Käsemann has quite rightly seen this chapter as central for understanding the
whole Gospel; thus, the subtitle of his book on *The Testament of Jesus: A Study of
the Gospel of John in the Light of Chapter 17.*

world, like Christ's own mission, bears the mark of divine love."[16] As Josef Kuhl expresses it, "When Jesus now sends his disciples into the world, then the same motif is guiding him as guided the Father at the sending of Jesus—that is, the motif of effecting the salvation of men and, finally, of glorifying the Father."[17]

The statement of Bultmann, then,[18] that "the world constantly has the possibility of being drawn into this circle of mutual love," appears to stand up; and the Christian may therefore be understood, in the Johannine literature, as being sent on a mission of love to the world.[19] It must be remembered, however, that this mission of love involves *only* the carrying of the gospel to the world, *not* unlimited care exercised toward one's fellow man. As long as the "neighbor" remains unconverted, unbelieving, remains "of the world," the Christian should hold himself apart from the neighbor. In 1 John 2:15–17 (to which Käsemann has already drawn our attention) this is made clear: "Do not love the world nor what is in the world . . . because everything that is in the world—the desire of the flesh and the desire of the eyes and the boastfulness of life [*bios*, not *zoē*]—is not of the Father but is of the world." With this holding oneself aloof from the world goes being hated by the world,[20] as John 15 repeatedly and 1 John 3:13 point out.

The Christian mission, then, is the carrying out of love beyond the bounds of the congregation. Jesus sends "the men whom [God] gave [him] out of the world" (John 17:6) "into the world" just as God had previously sent him (17:18); and he intends for them to "bear fruit" (15:8, 16). Thus, in the words of Josef Kuhl, "John sees the church as a missionary entity through and through; as a community, the justification of whose existence in the world lies in its carrying out the mission of salvation on which its Lord has sent it."[21] We must therefore understand clearly that the

---

16. Ibid., p. 61.
17. Kuhl, *Die Sendung Jesu*, p. 143.
18. Above, pp. 91 f.
19. Cf. further Preisker, *Das Ethos des Urchristentums*, p. 215.
20. The Johannine authors, however, always stop short of any mention of *hating the world*, a point less than clearly seen by Brown, *Gospel According to John*, p. 613, who compares the Johannine being hated by the world with the hatred of opponents attested in the Dead Sea Scrolls.
21. Kuhl, *Die Sendung Jesu*, p. 207.

"narrowing" to which Preisker referred does in fact allow for a certain kind of love beyond the congregation, but that the love that reaches beyond the congregation thinks of the welfare of the "world" only in terms of bringing the neighbor to faith—nothing else. The very existence of the church is "so that the world may believe that thou didst send me" (John 17:21), i.e., "that the world may know that thou didst send me and didst love them just as thou didst love me" (v. 23). Thus it becomes clear that "the carrying out of the revelation by Jesus and the community of his disciples is directed toward arousing faith, because precisely faith is the conditio sine qua non for the salvation of the cosmos."[22]

When one applies the question of contemporary relevance to this position, then it becomes immediately clear that the premise that the supreme and only good that one can do for one's neighbor is to bring him to faith in Jesus as the divine revealer sent from God, can be valid and relevant only for the church—can be valid and relevant, in fact, only for the church that accepts the Johannine position that Jesus *is* the divine revealer sent from God, who offers faith in the revelation as the present appropriating for oneself of eternal life. John 5:24 explains the matter perfectly: "He who hears my word and believes him who sent me has eternal life and does not come under judgment but has gone over from death to life."

In connection with love, the Johannine Jesus also sets unity before the church as the proper definition of its being.[23] "In order that all may be one," he prays for "believers," "just as thou, Father, art in me and I in thee, in order that they also may be in us, in order that the world may believe that thou didst send me" (17:21). The relation between the unity and love is seen plainly in the parallel between verse 23, "I in them and thou in me, in order that they may be completed in unity (*hen*), in order that the world may know . . . ," and verse 26, "in order that the love with which thou hast loved me may be in them and I in them." Jesus in them, love in them, unity—they are all the same. Thus, the concept of unity in the church adds nothing to the discussion;

22. Ibid., p. 170.
23. So also Furnish, *The Love Command*, p. 139. Käsemann, *Testament of Jesus*, p. 56, has perceptively, and correctly, noted the nearness of the Fourth Gospel to Ephesians in this regard.

its raison d'être is "that the world may believe" (17:21) or "know"
(17:23),[24] which is also the raison d'être of love in the church,
which is in fact the very raison d'être for the church itself.[25]
Ethically speaking, the same tunnel vision exists right through
the Gospel and Epistles of John; the supreme and only good that
one can do for one's fellow man is to witness to him so that he
may believe and in believing have life.

Within the church, however, the old rules apply. The old rules,
that is, about how the Christian is to treat his brother (formerly
neighbor). This is the second point given to the footwashing in
chapter 13 (the first point is that "only the man who accepts this
service has fellowship with [Jesus], remains united with him"[26]),
i.e., that "the disciple, for his part, is to render this kind of service
to his fellow disciple."[27] Thus Jesus explains, in John 13:14, "If
. . . I, the master and teacher, have washed your feet, you also
ought to wash one another's feet." This would appear to be meant
not literally, but symbolically, suggestively, so that "we have here
an anticipation of the exposition (in 13:34; 15:12) of the command of love."[28] The point would then be that no one is too good,
too proud, in too high a position to do whatever is needful for
the welfare of his fellow Christian. This is in any case the understanding placed on the love commandment in 1 John 3:16–18.
"In this we have known love," the writer explains, "that he laid
down his life for our benefit; and we ought to lay down our lives
for our brothers." (So also John 15:13.) Within the church, the
love commandment is absolute. As with the original commandment of Jesus of Nazareth to love one's neighbor as oneself, so
here there is no compromising, no place for considerations of one's
own welfare or even existence. "Whoever yet draws breath [*echēi
ton bion tou kosmou*] and sees his brother needing anything and
withholds his mercy from him, how can God's love abide in him?"

---

24. Cf. Feuillet, *Johannine Studies*, p. 159, who refers to the unity as "the chief
sign of credibility presented to men"; also Bultmann, *Gospel of John*, p. 514.
25. Cf. also the remarks of Dodd, *Interpretation of the Fourth Gospel*, pp. 195–97,
and of Helmut Koester, "History and Cult in the Gospel of John and in Ignatius
of Antioch," trans. Arthur Bellinzoni, *JThC* 1 (1965): 121 f.
26. Bultmann, *Gospel of John*, p. 468. See also Bultmann's excellent discussion on
the whole footwashing pericope, ibid., pp. 466–79.
27. Ibid., p. 474.
28. Ibid., p. 475.

continues 1 John. It is a crazy, dual way of behaving toward one's fellow men. The only concern with those outside the church is to bring them into the church, into the unity of faith and love that is the church; within the church, one gives everything for one's brother, whatever his need, willingly, selflessly, even to the giving up of life itself. How is this dual standard to be explained? The reason for the difference is that, within the church, the presence of the eschaton is affirmed.

Here is not the place to enter into extensive discussion over the issue of present and future eschatology in the Johannine literature. However the conjecture, first made by Bultmann, that statements of future eschatology in the Gospel of John give evidence of an *ecclesiastical redaction*[29] may finally be judged, there can be no doubt that the major emphasis in John lies on the eschaton as present in faith. Thus John 5:24 states flatly that the one who believes "has gone over [*metabebēken*—perfect] from death to life"; and the discussion between Jesus and Martha in 11:20–27 makes clear that to understand the statement, "Your brother will arise," as, "He will arise in the resurrection on the last day," is a misunderstanding. Jesus argues that he (Jesus) *is* "resurrection and life"; to prove what that means, he asks Martha if she believes, and, when she says that she does, he raises Lazarus from the dead! No more graphic illustration of Johannine present eschatology appears anywhere in the Gospel and Epistles. Not a little other evidence further confirms Bultmann's opinion that the future eschatology in the Gospel is to be laid to the hand of a redactor. One may note especially the refrain-like way in which present eschatology is reversed into future eschatology in chapter 6. Cf. 6:39, 40, 44.[30]

In faith, then, there *is* life. So John 5:24 states, "He who hears my word and believes him who sent me has eternal life." The longed for eternal life is in fact present where faith exists,[31] i.e., where there are those who believe, who are still "in the world" but not "of" it—in short, in the congregation of faith, in the

29. Ibid., passim.
30. Ibid., p. 219.
31. Bultmann, *Theology of the New Testament*, vol. 2, p. 78, refers to "transition into eschatological existence."

church. The eschaton, in other words, has in fact occurred where faith has occurred; or, as Bultmann puts it, "Precisely this is the community's task: to exist in the world as the eschatological community."[32] Thus, once again, ethics in the New Testament is inescapably linked to eschatology. In this case, the tension, the dialectical thinking produced in early Christianity—most notably in Paul's writings—as a result of the conviction that the Christian lived somehow no longer in the old age but not quite yet in the new, or in some way in both ages at once, has been resolved by dissolving the temporal understanding of eschatology into a concept of an "in" group (believers) and an "out" group (the "world").[33] Within the "in" group, within the church, the life that others awaited has already been made present in faith, so that there the absolute command to love may be made, with little or no need to elaborate on its meaning. The commandment is sufficiently explained in 1 John 3:16–18. The relation of members of this group to the "world" is not to be "of" it, which will imply that the "world" will hate the church. But the church can live with that situation, because it can view the "world" as the realm of darkness and lies from which believers are glad to have escaped, and because it has the guiding presence of the Spirit, which of course is denied to the "world."

On the question of the possible validity of such an ethics today, one should note first that this is precisely the ethics of the new fundamentalism. Claiming that Christians should not be concerned with war, poverty, racial inequities, and the rights of women (in other words, with those "worldly" issues), today's young fundamentalists devote their every energy to converting non-believers, to helping those who are "of the world" to believe and thus to escape the "world" for life in Christ or life in the Spirit. They often form small, tightly knit groups, more or less, indeed, hated by the "world," and provide comfort and various kinds of aid for one another. Whether the love that is practiced within such groups goes so far as "laying down one's life" for one's brother or sister (1 John 3:16) is certainly open to question, but

32. Bultmann, *Gospel of John*, p. 507.

33. On the dissolution of the temporal element in John, cf. further Bultmann, *Theology of the New Testament*, vol. 2, p. 79.

an attempt is made, in any case, to "love not in word or tongue but in deed and truth" (1 John 3:18). Precisely because such groups, however, now exist in sufficient abundance to be visible, perhaps the weakness and moral bankruptcy of the Johannine ethics can be seen more clearly. Here is not a Christianity that considers that loving is the same as fulfilling the law (Paul) or that the good Samaritan parable represents a demand (Luke) to stop and render even first aid to the man who has been robbed, beaten, and left there for dead. Johannine Christianity is interested only in whether he believes. "Are you saved, brother?" the Johannine Christian asks the man bleeding to death on the side of the road. "Are you concerned about your soul?" "Do you believe that Jesus is the one who came down from God?" "If you believe, you will have eternal life," promises the Johannine Christian, while the dying man's blood stains the ground.

VI

THE LATER EPISTLES[1]

AND THE APOCALYPSE

In general, one may observe that many of the tendencies already seen to be at work in the post-Pauline tradition are also at work in these writings.[2] Thus, as one might suspect, the love commandment has disappeared, being found in this collection only in James 2:8, where it stands alone, unexplained, unrelated to anything else in James. A dim memory of the love commandment is probably also to be seen in Heb. 10:24, where *agapē* is paralleled to good works, and perhaps in Heb. 6:10, where the congregation is lauded for having demonstrated *agapē* to God's account (or with respect to him) in having ministered, and in ministering, to the saints; although, whether the latter should be carried back ultimately to the love commandment would be impossible to decide. Love is made the crowning virtue (after *philadelphia*) in 2 Pet. 1:7, as in Col. 3:14; and the author of Revelation once lists *agapē* (2:19) as one in a list of Christian virtues and once chides the church at Ephesus for having forsaken its first love (2:4 f.), after which he calls the church back to its former works. Thus, *agapē* seems again to be paralleled to good works, as in Heb. 10:24.

---

1. Hebrews, Jude, 2 Peter, and James. Some of the writings that might properly be termed "later Epistles" have, of course, already been treated in chaps. 4 and 5.

2. For a further comprehensive discussion of the interrelatedness of the ethics in this literature, the Johannine literature, and the deutero-Pauline literature cf. especially Herbert Preisker, *Das Ethos des Urchristentums*, pp. 195–219, and Rudolf Bultmann, *Theology of the New Testament*, vol. 2, pp. 218–31. Important and thorough as these two works are in their understanding of New Testament ethics, they both display what is, in my opinion, a deficiency in the way they deal with the literature of the later New Testament period. The practice of both authors of lumping the later literature together tends to obscure certain important differences; and it is for this reason that I have chosen to deal with this literature on a more individual basis.

What is new in this literature is that *agapē* acquires a meaning that has nothing to do with ethics. Jude 2 offers the wish that mercy, peace, and love may abound to the readers. Here, then, *agapē* appears to refer to the desired state of being of the Christian, who finds himself beset with the problems facing early Christianity—that is, the author wishes that the readers' ship may sail from the troubled waters of doctrinal conflicts into the calm waters of mercy, peace, and love. Finally, the plural *agapai* appears, referring to the Lord's supper: Jude 12 and 2 Pet. 2:13.

Along with the loss of the love commandment, of course, goes the loss of imminent eschatology. Only Revelation, with its burning imminence, is an exception (for the imminence, cf. 6:11; 22:10–12; for the burning, cf. passim). What is especially interesting for Revelation is that the imminent eschatology is present, whereas the love commandment is not, except for the colorless mention of *agapē* in two places, noted above. This is due to the special character of the apocalyptic in Revelation, which will be discussed below where the book is examined individually. Elsewhere in this literature, however, the imminence is gone. Heb. 10:25 drags in the idea of imminence as one more reason (*tosoutōi mallon*) for not neglecting to go to church, but it is clear that the author is searching around for a reason. When he can find no other, he reminds his readers (hearers) that the Day is drawing near. *Agapē* was mentioned in the preceding verse, but the author makes no connection between the two, although it may well be that the close juxtaposition of love and imminent eschatology here reveals the strength of the tradition associating the two. The reason the author of Hebrews is basically disinterested in imminent eschatology, of course, is that he by and large has replaced that view with a two-worlds view and, in the heritage of Plato's thought, thinks of the heavenly world as the real one (cf. especially 10:1–18). How he puts the temporal transcendence of eschatology neatly together with spatial transcendence is seen in 4:11a, "Hasten, therefore, to enter" (temporal) "into that rest" (spatial). The language of entering the (coming) Kingdom of God has therefore been shifted over into the language of going to heaven.

In James, imminent eschatology is adduced as a justification, somewhat surprisingly, of patience.[3] The author counsels patience in 5:7 and cites the example of the farmer who waits for the harvest. Then, however, he encourages his readers by adding, "For the Parousia of the Lord has drawn near [*ēggiken*]," and he supports this further by admonishing in verse 9 that "the judge stands before the doors." The use of imminent eschatology here is analogous to Paul's use of it in Rom. 13:11–14; only the difference is that there Paul reminded his readers of the nearness of the coming of the Day of the Lord in order to give them the courage really to carry out the love commandment in the present. James, however, reminds *his* readers of the nearness for an inverse reason, to encourage their patience! The reasoning is actually somewhat circular; since it is the delay of the Parousia that makes patience necessary, patience then becomes a virtue, and the eschatology becomes its justification, just as it may be for any other desired ethical action. In any case, one hardly gets the impression that imminent eschatology is a live, motivating force for the author of James. All James is interested in is supporting the injunction to patience as a virtue, in spite of his use of the (inherited) language of imminence. He clearly gives this away when he cites as examples of patience, not Jesus or the apostles, but the *prophets* (v. 10) and *Job* (v. 11)—personages of the distant past, who certainly did not have the time of their patience cut short by the coming of the Lord![4] The author had earlier (4:14) referred to the fact that people who made plans for tomorrow were those "who do not know about tomorrow." This is not, however, a reference to eschatology, but rather a thought that "is expressed in the most different poetic and paraenetic texts."[5]

Jude 18 reminds that "the Apostles of the Lord . . . said" that there would be a last day, but Jude uses the saying of the

3. Not at all surprising, however, when one views James against the background not of the New Testament, but of the tradition of Hellenistic Jewish homilies. Cf. Hartwig Thyen, *Der Stil der Jüdisch-Hellenistischen Homilie*, FRLANT, N.F. 47 (Göttingen, 1955), pp. 106 f.

4. Hans Windisch, *Die katholischen Briefe*, p. 31, however, takes the eschatological language of 5:1–3 at face value and thinks that, in James's view, "the end time . . . has already broken in."

5. Martin Dibelius, *Der Brief des Jakobus*, p. 277, the English translation of which is soon to be published by Fortress Press in the Hermeneia series.

Apostles only to prove that the situation of the present time—
presence of "scoffers"—was foretold, not to emphasize that the end
is at hand. The eschatology is strictly inherited *didachē*, and the
author has no idea what it means. If imminent eschatology has in
Jude become finally and completely meaningless, it is in Jude's
counterpart, 2 Peter, that one finds imminence entirely explained
away. "One day with the Lord," counsels 2 Pet. 3:8, perhaps in
reliance on Ps. 90:4, "is like a thousand years and a thousand
years like one day." The whole passage, 3:1–10, makes the same
point. The author does continue to look forward to the coming
of the Lord, especially in 3:9–12, but one must wonder why (v. 11
no doubt gives the answer, the eschatology must still be brought
forward as the irreducible sanction for "what sort [of people] you
ought to be"), and one is really not surprised to find 2 Peter
seeming to refer, in 1:16, to the fact that the Apostles were eye-
witnesses *already* to the coming (Parousia) of the Lord, or looking
forward, in 1:19, to the time when "day breaks and the sun[6] rises
in your hearts."[7]

Imitatio Christi is to be found in Heb. 12:3, but 13:7 counsels
imitating the faith of the leaders, and James 5:10 urges taking the
prophets as examples.

One of the most perplexing characteristics of the ethics of the
later Pauline tradition, as was seen in chapter 4, was the equating
of Christian ethics with general good morality, while at the same
time maintaining that Christians are different from others precisely because of their ethics. That note is, in part, in evidence in
these later Epistles. Heb. 13 and James, both of which are examples of the kind of paraenesis to be found in Hellenistic Jewish
homilies (on this point see the individual discussions below), for
the most part advocate an ethics that is not to be distinguished

6. *Phōsphoros,* "light bearer." Windisch, *Die katholischen Briefe,* p. 90, notes, "For
phōsphoros one would like to think of the rising sun, but only the meaning 'morn-
ing star' is attested"; nevertheless, whatever is attested in other literature, the
parallelism between *hēmera* and *phōsphoros* in this verse forces one to the conclusion that the sun is here meant.
7. This *en tais kardiais hymōn* of 1:19 probably also reveals what the author had
in mind when he referred in 1:11 to "the eternal Kingdom"; i.e., the phrase seems
to be used more in the sense of Hebrews than as explained by J. N. D. Kelly, *A
Commentary on the Epistles of Peter and Jude,* p. 310, who writes that, in 2 Pet.
1:11, "the kingdom is no longer thought of as coming to men, still less as already
present . . . ; it lies in the future and is equated with the endless blessedness upon
which believers who hold fast will enter at the Parousia."

from Hellenistic Jewish or Stoic ethics, although Hebrews, somewhat like 1 Pet. 2:13–3:7, provides Christianizing sanctions (James
does not). Neither Heb. 13 nor James, however, lays any emphasis
on the other point found in the literature of the Pauline tradition,
that Christians, by following the ethics advocated, give evidence
of their distinctiveness as Christians. Exactly the same situation is
to be observed in 2 Peter, so that Hans Windisch, at the opening
of an excursus on "Hellenistic Piety in II Peter," states, "The
whole period [2 Pet. 1:] 3 and 4 (cf. also 5–7) is filled with views
and phrases of Hellenistic piety."[8] However, 2 Peter also makes
no specific attempt to show that Christians who attain to the
virtues listed there are different from everyone else.

James 1:27, "to keep oneself unstained from the world," and
4:4, which equates friendship with the world with enmity toward
God, could conceivably be thought to echo the idea found to
some degree in the pastoral Epistles that the Christian should
avoid contact with non-Christians. More likely, however, we have
here in James only the mere general advice not to adopt "worldly"
habits.

A catalog of vices is found in Rev. 21:8.

Finally, all the present writings take up, in one way or another,
the deutero-Pauline admonition to hold on to the received faith
or teachings. This is probably most pronounced in Hebrews,
where the ethics consists almost entirely of advising "holding fast
the confession"; one may note especially Heb. 2:1; 3:12; 10:23,
and 35 f.[9] Likewise, James 1:3 views the "testing of your faith"
positively; and Jude 3 appeals for the readers to "struggle for the
faith once delivered to the saints." This note provides, then, the
theme for the whole Epistle of Jude (cf. again v. 20) and, consequently, for 2 Pet. 3:1 ff. as well. Revelation rounds out the picture when the church at Pergamum (2:13) and the church at
Philadelphia (3:8) are praised, respectively, for not denying the
Lord's faith and for keeping his word while not denying his name.

This collection of writings, then, gives not a little evidence of
similarity, where ethics is concerned, to the later Epistles of the
Pauline tradition, although differing nuances within those simi-

8. Windisch, *Die katholischen Briefe*, p. 85.
9. Cf. further below, pp. 106–109.

larities have been noted. It remains now to examine these tracts in their separateness and distinctiveness.

The structure of the Epistle to the Hebrews, as nearly all commentators agree, is one of alternating theological and paraenetic sections.[10] Furthermore, it is certainly the case, as Otto Michel asserts, that "the crowning point of the theological thought lies in the paraenetic portions";[11] otherwise, as he observes, Hebrews would only be an interesting "theological treatment." The theological sections are, in other words, leading somewhere, and that somewhere is discovered in the paraenetic sections. Unfortunately for our interest here, however, these paraenetic sections have precious little to say about one's ethical dealings with one's fellow men or with one's world but deal rather almost exclusively with the strictly religious ethical concern that the congregation "hold fast" to its "confession."[12] Thus, 2:1 right away advises that "it is necessary for us to pay attention much more to the things we have heard, lest we deviate"; and, in like vein, 10:23 offers the admonition, "Let us hold fast the confession of hope unchangingly." "Confidence," therefore, and "endurance" (10:35 f.) become principal virtues of the congregation; and sin can be equated with disbelief, as in 3:12, where one finds the phrase, "an evil [ponēra] heart of disbelief."[13]

It would appear that the author of Hebrews thinks of "love and good works" (mentioned twice, both times together, in 6:10 and 10:24) as a subdivision of the broader category of keeping the faith.[14] Thus, after stating in 6:10 that God would not be so un-

10. Cf. the extensive discussion of the structure in Otto Michel, *Der Brief an die Hebräer*, pp. 21–36. Jean Héring, however, *The Epistle to the Hebrews*, trans. A. W. Heathcote and P. J. Allcock (Epworth, 1970), p. xvi, divides the letter into a didactic (chaps. 1–10) and a paraenetic (chaps. 11–13) section.
11. Michel, *Brief an die Hebräer*, p. 27.
12. Ibid., p. 80, also reminds that this "keeping the faith" will likely include suffering; cf. Heb. 12:1–11.
13. Ernst Käsemann, *Das wandernde Gottesvolk*, pp. 26 f., also makes this point, as does C. Spicq, *L'Épître aux Hébreux*, vol. 1, pp. 131, 285 f.
14. Similarly also Wolfgang Nauck, "Zum Aufbau des Hebräerbriefes," in *Judentum, Urchristentum, Kirche, Festschrift J. Jeremias* (Berlin, 1964[2]), p. 206. Spicq, also, in *L'Épître aux Hébreux*, vol. 2, p. 416, sees that remaining "faithful to the Christ, to his person and to his doctrine, . . . provides the foundation of the moral

just as to "overlook your work and the love which you showed with respect to him," he goes on to urge the readers, in verse 12, to become "imitators of those who, through faith and patience, are inheriting the promises." Clearer still is 10:23 f. Here, after urging holding "fast the confession of faith," the author adds, "and let us give attention to one another to incite love and good works." To keep the faith is the Christian's general task and the principal admonition of Hebrews. Love and good works make up one—not unimportant—aspect of that.

What the good works are surfaces only in chapter 13, but it is worth pausing here to note that the only place in the whole homily where the author mentions anything like an imminent eschatology is just here in 10:25, where he states that the congregation's coming together—and one should probably understand also the previously mentioned keeping the faith and inciting love and good works—are all the more important as the Christians see "the Day [of the Lord] drawing near."[15] Thus the author who, more than any other New Testament writer, transforms temporal into spatial transcendence, who transforms the idea of a future time of salvation into the idea of a heavenly sphere of salvation, cannot avoid, where it is a matter of the ethics of the Kingdom, of *agapē*, adding that the time is short.[16] Here, just like Paul, this author who is in so many other ways quite distinct from Paul instinctively, as it were, reaches for the eschatological undergirding when he reminds his congregation to love. The virtues he is going to spell out in chapter 13 do not need this eschatological undergirding at all; they are quite conceivable in a continuing world, and our author certainly means the virtues of chapter 13 to be examples of love (cf. 13:1: "Let brotherly love [*philadelphia*] abide"). Nevertheless, the tradition that one is freed to love—to love in the total and completely selfless way which was earlier meant by *agapē*—because the time is short, is so strong that the author must

---

teaching" of Hebrews. He then seems to slip, however, when, commenting on 13:16, he suggests that the Christian serves God *both* with his lips *and* with his works (p. 430).

15. Gerd Theissen, *Untersuchungen zum Hebräerbrief*, pp. 90 f., finds most occurrences of future eschatology in Hebrews in the paraenetic portions.

16. On this point, see especially James Moffatt, *A Critical and Exegetical Commentary on the Epistle to the Hebrews* and Theissen, *Untersuchungen zum Hebräerbrief*, passim.

bring it in here, even though he nowhere else gives the slightest indication that the idea of an imminent end is at all important for him.

At the end of his missive, then, our author gives, in some detail, what he considers to be leading or particularly apropos examples of the love and good works to which he had twice previously referred. That this final chapter is not a loose appendage but is rather the logical conclusion of the homily,[17] stating in clear and practical terms what behavior is implied in keeping the faith, should be clear from at least two observations. In the first place, the "let brotherly love abide," which is the heading of the chapter, likely intends to take up the "love and good works" of 6:10 and 10:24 (that *agapē* and *philadelphia* may be more or less interchangeable in late first century Christianity has already been seen in the discussion of 1 Peter). Then, too, *imitatio fidei*, which already in 6:12 followed upon the mention of "work and love" in 6:10 (and was also alluded to in 12:3), is urged upon the readers in 13:7, just after the brief list of ethical admonitions in verses 2–5. When, then, 13:9 goes on to advise, "Do not be borne away by many and strange teachings" (i.e., "hold on to the confession"), we see that we have the same pattern here as in 6:10–12 (and, reversed, in 10:23 f.), the only difference being that, appropriately at the end of the "letter," the loving works are specified in a paraenesis. Chapter 13, then, intends to spell out the practical implications of keeping the faith, which is the principal ethical interest of the author of Hebrews.

The theological reason the author of Hebrews gives for making "keeping the faith" the primary ethical demand is that this is the way to attain the object of the Christian hope.[18] This idea appears in one way or another throughout Hebrews, but one may cite especially the discussion of the "rest" in chapters 3 and 4 and the discourse on "faith" in chapter 11. Although this theme is mentioned in chapter 13 (v. 14: "We are seeking the coming

---

17. Michel, *Brief an die Hebräer*, p. 479, and Spicq, *L'Épître aux Hébreux*, vol. 2, pp. 415 f. have also seen this correctly, *pace* Moffatt, *Hebrews*, p. 224.

18. Käsemann, *Das wandernde Gottesvolk*, p. 20, makes this point especially well and shows the contrast to Paul's understanding of faith. Cf. also Michel, *Brief an die Hebräer*, p. 250.

[city]"), it is hardly there made the general foundation of the paraenesis; rather, the individual items of the paraenesis seem to be considered (1) as examples of *philadelphia* and (2) each to have its own individual justification. This would seem to show that, much as the author of Hebrews has sought to make it appear that the paraenesis grows integrally out of the demand to "hold fast the confession," he nevertheless relies only on inherited paraenetic material[19] which already in the tradition carries with it its own justification(s) and cannot be altogether coordinated with our author's basic ethical premise. That is to say, the individual items of chapter 13 are there, not because the author has reflected on the ethical implications of his theological argument and come up with them, but rather because he already knows that they are the right things to do, already knows this because it is stock Christian teaching.

It is not clear whether, in giving individual justifications for each item in the paraenesis, the author is relying on tradition or is himself providing the traditional admonitions with his own justifications. Since the individual justifications do not at all (e.g., v. 4: "God will judge fornicators and adulterers") or only loosely (e.g., v. 5: "I will surely neither forsake you nor leave you in the lurch") relate to the author's primary ethical interest, one may probably assume the former. Michel thinks, for example, that "the final clause v. 4b [above] has the style of a prophetic regulation (like 1 Cor. 15:50)."[20] Although the clause is not in the form of a tenet of holy law, Michel could well be right.[21] In any case, chapter 13 does not succeed in presenting a *paradigm* for Christian living based on a consistent theological foundation but only gives more or less random *examples*, each with its own foundation.

---

19. On this point, cf. Michel, *Brief an die Hebräer*, Moffatt, *Hebrews*, and Hans Windisch, *Der Hebräerbrief*, HNT (Tübingen, 1931²), all on chap. 13.

20. Michel, *Brief an die Hebräer*, p. 482.

21. One would have to assume an original prophetic saying something like, "Whoever is a fornicator or adulterer, God will judge him," where the normal correspondence of the sin mentioned in the protasis with the punishment decreed in the apodosis would have been given up, for the sake of sense, for the more general word "judge." Verse 4b would then be not the prophetic pronouncement of holy law itself, but rather a literary version of the same, which has been secondarily coupled as a justification or sanction, probably prior to its use by our author, with the admonition to keep marriage honorable.

It is not possible to derive any further ethical guidance from chapter 13.

Not that there is anything wrong with the examples! Such behavior as properly caring for strangers, reminding oneself what it is like to be a prisoner and acting toward prisoners accordingly, and keeping marriage an honored institution are fine virtues with which most people from that time to this would agree. But just in this agreement one sees that the author of Hebrews finds himself, ethically speaking, still in the same Christian ethical tradition inaugurated by the authors of Colossians and Ephesians—that is, Christian ethics is equated with good citizenship. Whatever the theology, we seem now to have reached a stage in the development of early Christianity when the ethical implications of the theology are always the same: Do what is right, what is good, what everyone knows to be right and good. The particular examples, of course, are often, if not always, called forth by the particular situation,[22] as will be the case here with the twice mentioned advice about those in charge (vv. 7 and 17). Michel evaluates this general character of "the good" positively,[23] realizing, however, neither that one no longer needs Christianity in order to propose such an ethics nor that Hebrews has given no real leads at all (contrary to Rom. 12, which Michel cites as analogous to Heb. 13!) for defining "the good."

Once the ethical tradition, however, becomes locked onto this beam of doing the obvious good, it is on a collision course with obscurity. Having lost the reality of the expectation of the imminent end (the memory of which is nevertheless so strong in the ethical tradition that, as we have seen, it still struggles to the surface in the context of the now dead love commandment), Christian ethics is now altogether awash. It lacks direction, motivation, even a raison d'être. The New Testament will yet provide us with one noble, albeit fleeting attempt to lift Christian ethics out of this lethargy and to give it new life as well as new direction and a new rationale; but we need yet to examine three other Christian writings in the New Testament before taking up the matter of the ill-fated tract in which that case is found.

22. So also Michel, *Brief an die Hebräer*, p. 478.
23. Ibid., p. 539.

JUDE AND 2 PETER

It is fairly widely recognized that 2 Peter relies in large measure on Jude—that is, that Jude has served as extensive source material for 2 Peter, although the author of 2 Peter has not slavishly copied Jude.[24] This will be assumed here and not argued further.

There is, unfortunately, little to be said about the ethics of these Epistles and the bases for the ethics that has not already been said above in the introductory remarks to this chapter. The author of Jude begins (v. 3) by appealing to his readers "to struggle for the faith once delivered to the saints." There follows a brief but imaginative denunciation of teachers of false doctrine, and verses 20–23 then, in conclusion, expand somewhat further on the theme of "struggling for the faith."[25] This same argument is then taken up by 2 Peter, which fleshes it out still further. The only material, however, which the author of 2 Peter has added to this appeal to struggle for the faith which is of significance for our ethical interest is the ascending list of virtues in 1:5–7: "Put forth every effort to produce in your faith virtue, and in virtue knowledge, and in knowledge self-control, and in self-control endurance, and in endurance piety, and in piety brotherly love [philadelphia], and in brotherly love, love [agapē]." Only the first and last items in the list (faith and love) are specifically Christian, however,[26] and even these are unrelated to anything else in the Epistle and are unexplained. The author makes no attempt to justify the existence of one or another item in the list. He only informs his readers that "when these things belong and abound to you, they make you neither useless nor unfruitful as regards the knowledge of our Lord Jesus Christ" (1:8), and that "when you do these things you will never fall" (v. 10). There thus appears to be no criterion at all for placing certain virtues on the list; it is just that, given a list of more or less Christian virtues, one aspires to them in order to be saved. Windisch also notes, quite correctly, that there is no logic to the list, "for piety in-

24. For thorough evidence on this point, cf. Werner Georg Kümmel, *Introduction to the New Testament*, p. 303.
25. The "love of God" in v. 21 is probably subjective genitive. In any case, it has nothing to do with ethics.
26. On the Hellenistic character of the list, see Windisch, *Die katholischen Briefe*, pp. 85 f.

cludes faith and knowledge and is really the central function;
self-control and endurance belong to virtue, as well as brotherly
love, which can hardly be distinguished from love."[27]

In addition to the remarks made at the first of this chapter on
the eschatology of 2 Peter, one may note here further, in conclusion, that eschatology is formally, at least, still hooked to an ethical imperative in 3:11 f., although there is nothing in these two
verses to imply that the nearness of the end calls forth a particular
ethics.[28]

REVELATION

Most of the ethical clues in this Christian apocalypse are to be
found in chapters 2 f., the letters to the seven churches. Rev. 2:2
refers to the "works" and "labor" and "endurance" of the church
at Ephesus but seems to define these virtues as witch-hunting for
false apostles and excommunicating evil persons (which probably
mean the same thing). Similar virtues are attributed to the church
at Thyatira (2:19), where the list contains "works," "love," "faith,"
"service," and "endurance." Taking "service" as the equivalent
of the previous "labor," one may thus see that the author has
merely repeated the list of 2:2, Christianizing it by the addition
of love and faith. Again, excommunication of a false prophetess,
one Jezebel (2:20), is also referred to with approval. The importance of the Ephesian church's endurance is then especially emphasized in 2:3; and 2:4 f., as was noted above, reminds the church
of its former love and calls it back to its first works, which appear
to mean the love. In the letters to the churches, then, at Smyrna
(2:10), at Pergamum (2:13), and at Philadelphia (3:8), holding
firm to the faith is held out as the important ethical characteristic.
Further, the scolding of the church at Laodicea for being "luke-
warm" (3:15 f.) apparently also refers to the relative "heat" of
that church's faith.

Following the "letters," in the body of the Apocalypse only not
worshiping the beast (ch. 13), male virginity (14:4), and a general
list of sins (21:8—unbelief, murder, et al.) may be noted as examples of ethics. Finally, 22:11, "Let the evil person still do iniquity,

27. Ibid., p. 86.
28. On the eschatology of 2 Peter, cf. especially Kelly, *Peter and Jude*, p. 310.

. . . and let the just person still do righteousness," means, coming as it does just after the statement in verse 10 that "the time is near at hand," that the end is too near for anyone to change.

It is this last statement, which assumes that a change of behavior could not now be effected, that lets us see why the Apocalypse has so little—nothing of lasting or fundamental value—to say about ethics, and why this is the case precisely in that New Testament work which has the most burningly imminent eschatology of all, whereas we have become accustomed to associate imminent eschatology elsewhere in the New Testament with a strong ethical demand and especially with a truly living love commandment. The reasón is that Revelation, reintroducing imminent eschatology at a time when (as far as we can tell from other New Testament and patristic writings) such an eschatology within Christianity was already drawing its last breath—if it had not already expired altogether—that Revelation in doing this is as foreign to the preaching of Jesus and the letters of Paul as is Jude or 2 Peter; indeed, it is more so.

Jesus had understood that the nearness of the righteous God, and Paul that the nearness of the Lord's coming implied total obedience to the love commandment in its radical self-disregard. At a time, however, when that view had faded, when the radical implications of the love commandment were no longer recognized and the commandment itself was passing into obscurity, and when imminent eschatology was remembered only in a formal way as providing a sanction—a last ditch sanction—for ethics, it was possible to attempt[29] to reintroduce imminent eschatology as authentic Christian expectation, this time with all the apocalyptic imagery and trappings so foreign to Jesus and Paul, and without relating that expectation to the necessity of living as eschatological community, as if already in the Kingdom.[30] The difference, there-

29. The attempt was never successful. Cf. the discussion in Kümmel, *Introduction to the New Testament*, pp. 331 f.
30. Elisabeth Fiorenza, "The Eschatology and Composition of the Apocalypse," *CBQ* 30 (1968): 537–69, seems correctly to have interpreted this use of apocalyptic in Revelation as an attempt to "comfort the persecuted Christian community" (p. 569). In this light, the assumption of 22:11 that it is too late to change is quite understandable. So also Wilhelm Thüsing, "Die theologische Mitte der Weltgerichts-visionen in der Johannesapokalypse," *Trierer theologische Zeitschrift* 77 (1968): 2. Thüsing completely overlooks, however (p. 16), the qualitative difference between the imminent expectation of Revelation and that of Jesus and Paul and emphasizes

fore, between the imminent eschatology of Jesus and Paul, on the one hand, and the Christian apocalyptic of Revelation, on the other, is a difference that may be expressed in terms of internal and external, or between existential and superficial. That is to say that Jesus and Paul laid emphasis on *how one must now be*, whereas Revelation only barely mentions the importance of Christian being, thinks primarily of keeping the faith and enduring,[31] and regards the time between the writing of the work and the end as a time of a *cosmic drama which one may view*. In the words of Akira Satake, "The attitude of the congregation is in this respect extremely passive."[32]

It is this *retreat from the ethical dimension* that is the basic evil of the Apocalypse. One might make the same charge, of course, against Jude and 2 Peter, and perhaps against Hebrews as well, but the difference between those tracts and Revelation is that they reckon with continuing Christian existence in the world, whereas Revelation does not. As long as Christians view the world as a place where they expect to continue to be, there is always the possibility, even when ethical interests are neglected, that a concern for one's fellow man and for the world can spring up again simply out of a perception of the needs that exist (which did in fact happen in one place in the New Testament, as we have yet to see), although a certain group of writers may have their senses dulled to ethical responsibility, may—having lost the ethics of the Kingdom along with the expectation of it—not see that continued existence in the world and among other human beings has its own ethical implications. Such a possibility, however, is excluded for Revelation; for the author expects the end soon and views the end as a time of the release of the church from the evils that beset

---

that both Jesus and the Apocalypse proclaim "that God's reign and realm have drawn near." The differences are then further buried when (Thüsing, "Die Vision des 'Neuen Jerusalem' [Apk. 21, 1–22, 5] als Verheissung und Gottesverkündigung," *Trierer theologische Zeitschrift* 77 [1968]: 17–34), with the aid of both allegorical and forced interpretations, Thüsing suddenly states that both Jesus and Revelation propose that the Christian's relation to the world is "service toward the brothers and sisters" (p. 32)—a statement for which Revelation gives not the first foundation.

31. Also correctly seen by Károly Karner, "Gegenwart und Endgeschichte in der Offenbarung des Johannes," *ThLZ* 93 (1968): 646 f.

32. Akira Satake, *Die Gemeindeordnung in der Johannesapokalypse*, Wissenschaftliche Monographien zum Alten und Neuen Testament, 21 (Neukirchen-Vluyn, 1966), p. 35.

it, as well as a time of vengeance. It is unfortunate that we are today experiencing a revival of just the kind of Christianity found in Revelation; but this revival has its ironically fortunate side in that it permits one to see with all clarity the degree to which such a position is ethically destitute. When persons today consciously and deliberately reject all obligation to help to seek to overcome the social, international, and individual problems of our time and insist that such problems are not the concern of the individual because Jesus is coming soon, we have the ultimate retreat from ethical responsibility. To the degree that the Apocalypse itself contributes to such views today, its existence and its place in the canon are, in the fullest sense of the word, evil.

JAMES

The Epistle of James presents the interpreter, at the outset, with certain peculiarities. For one thing, it is under no circumstances an epistle at all, but rather, from first to last (except for the epistolary opening), paraenesis—"small groups of aphorisms or even separate aphorisms [giving ethical instruction], which occasionally are connected by means of catchwords, but also often show no kind of recognizable connection."[33] James is therefore in this respect unique in the New Testament. Then there is the matter of whether James is even a Christian writing at all and not, rather, simply Hellenistic Jewish paraenesis.[34] Nevertheless, in spite of all the evidence of parallels from Hellenistic Jewish paraenetic literature, James was certainly written by someone who considered himself a Christian—that is, a church member and probably a church leader.

Martin Dibelius, although he is able in the case of almost every single item of the paraenesis in James to show that there is at least a possibility of Hellenistic Jewish origin, nevertheless is clear that

33. Kümmel, *Introduction to the New Testament*, p. 287, in reliance on Dibelius, *Brief des Jakobus*, passim, but especially pp. 13–23, "The Literary *Gattung* of the Epistle of James." Dibelius summarizes, pp. 16 f., "*We may therefore designate the 'Epistle' of James*, after examining its literary character in all its parts, *as paraenesis*. Under paraenesis we thereby understand a text which puts one-after-another admonitions of generally ethical content."
34. For a complete discussion of this problem and the various solutions that have been put forward, cf. Kümmel, *Introduction to the New Testament*, pp. 285–91, and Dibelius, *Brief des Jakobus*, pp. 23–43, 67–69, and passim.

James is a Christian work. Thus, for example, the phrase *parousia tou kyriou* (coming of the Lord) in 5:8 could be Jewish and not Christian,[35] but evidence for such an eschatological use of the word *parousia* in Jewish texts is meager and uncertain. The clearest and strongest argument, however, for the original Christianity of James has to do with the discussion of faith and works in 2:14–26. Such a discussion of the relative merits of faith and works, argues Dibelius, is *"certainly not conceivable without Paul's having before publicized the solution, 'faith, not works.' "*[36] Thus Dibelius concludes that the author is, at the earliest, a Christian of the second generation. On this evidence, then, James may be taken to be originally Christian, even though the origin of most of the material in the tract is Hellenistic Judaism (Dibelius), or even if James is a Christian revision of an earlier single Hellenistic Jewish work, as some have argued. The case need not be debated further here. The issue to which we must direct our attention here is, then, not the origin of the individual items of the paraenesis but the *way in which they are used in this work*.

Dibelius, whose commentary has the general effect of making it appear that there is no rhyme or reason to the choice of the individual items of the paraenesis in James, is not unconcerned with this issue. In his discussion of James 2:15 f., where the author argues that faith must produce good works in order to validate itself, Dibelius takes James's example of good works—helping the poor—to be not accidental but rather to reveal a particular interest of the author.[37] The possibility, however, of occasionally discovering the particular interest of the author does not lead Dibelius to any general conclusion about the author's theology or ethical principles; rather, in his opinion, the eclectic character of

35. Ibid., pp. 288 f.

36. Ibid., p. 220; cf. also the summary statements on the Christianity of James on p. 39. Dibelius is followed by Kümmel, *Introduction to the New Testament*, p. 289; cf. also Windisch, *Die katholischen Briefe*, pp. 3 f., 35 f. A number of other writers, of course, also advance Christian authorship for the tract. For a full discussion of the problem of determining the authorship of James, see the appropriate sections of Dibelius, *Brief des Jakobus*, and also of Windisch, *Die katholischen Briefe*, and Kümmel, *Introduction to the New Testament*. One should especially note that the older work of Arnold Meyer, *Das Rätsel des Jacobusbriefes*, although advancing the thesis that James was originally a Jewish letter of Jakob to his twelve sons that was then slightly revised by a Christian writer, nevertheless comes to a conclusion identical to that of Dibelius on the issue of the relationship between James and Paul. Cf. Meyer, ibid., p. 306.

37. Dibelius, *Brief des Jakobus*, p. 188.

the paraenesis prevents discovering the "spiritual situation of the author." Thus "the paraenesis takes on a certain internationalism and interconfessionalism, for ethical imperatives by no means need always express the particular faith in whose service they stand."[38] Dibelius's thorough and extensive demonstration of the *eclectic* character of the paraenesis that is James and of the way in which the individual items of the paraenesis are *independent* has been widely if not universally accepted by New Testament scholars. Nevertheless, a certain undercurrent of doubt has continued to run through the scholarly community on the issue of whether there is a discernible theme or particular theological orientation that may be found behind this collection of paraenetic materials.[39]

The most extensive attempt, since Dibelius's commentary, to find an underlying theme in James has been that of Georg Eichholz.[40] Eichholz proceeds by following Dibelius in the latter's analysis of the relation between James 2:14 ff. and Rom. 4. He agrees with Dibelius that the argument of James here presupposes Paul's earlier solution of "faith, not works,"[41] but he then wishes to go beyond Dibelius in insisting that James takes up "Pauline formulas."[42] To be sure, James does not understand the true profundity of the Pauline solution,[43] but rather argues against a Paul who is known only à la certain formulas.[44] That is to say

38. Ibid., p. 36.

39. Attempts to find such a theme have also, in large part, been motivated by the *canonical* problem that James stands opposed to Paul on the important issue of faith and works. The theological issue of the canon, which has been discussed briefly above (pp. 88–90), is peripheral to the issue of the ethics of James itself, and will not be treated further here.

40. Georg Eichholz, *Jakobus und Paulus* and idem, *Glaube und Werke bei Paulus und Jakobus*. A quite similar position had earlier been taken by Werner Bieder, "Christliche Existenz nach dem Zeugnis des Jakobusbriefes," *Theologische Zeitschrift* 5 (1949): 93–113. There is also, of course, the older view of Meyer, *Rätsel*, that James is a Christianized version of a Jewish letter of Jacob to his twelve sons.

41. Eichholz, *Jakobus und Paulus*, pp. 36 f.; Dibelius, *Brief des Jakobus*, p. 220, quoted above.

42. Eichholz, *Jakobus und Paulus*, p. 37.

43. Ibid., p. 41; cf. Dibelius, *Brief des Jakobus*, p. 219. Dibelius here correctly observes that "it is impossible that the author would have opposed Romans in this way *if he had read and understood it in a fundamental way*" (emphasis mine). Why does he then not consider the possibility that James had *not* so read and understood Paul, when it was Paul's fate to be misunderstood (as he elsewhere notes; cf. below, pp. 118 f.) ?

44. Eichholz refers to "ein *formelhaft gewordener Paulus*" in *Jakobus und Paulus*, p. 38. Cf. Windisch, *Die katholischen Briefe*, p. 20, who states that James does not know that his opponent may rely on Paul's concept of saving faith.

that James argues, not against the true position of Paul himself, but rather against a false understanding of certain Pauline formulas. Eichholz puts the difference between Paul and James this way: "*Because* Paul is dealing with man's *true obedience* he focuses all attention on *faith*, and *because* James is dealing with *complete obedience* he insists without compromise on *works*."[45]

Dibelius had been very careful to draw the line between a position that merely presupposed, in a general way, Paul's earlier solution and a conscious attack against an admittedly misunderstood Paul. He was persuaded that James fell into the former category. He raised the possibility that James may be directed against "rotten, inactive Christianity" that in some way goes back to Paul, but concluded that even this "possibility is by no means certain," since James is writing "not as polemicist against directions and parties that are present, but as teacher" who merely has observed that some Christians behave in the way described in 2:14 ff.[46]

Dibelius goes to great length to point out that James's use of Abraham, in 2:14 ff., as an example of the ideal of faith *and* works is not a conscious or deliberate attempt to revise the use of Abraham as an example of faith in Rom. 4, but rather grows out of existing Jewish tradition about Abraham as an example of faith credited as righteousness.[47] Eichholz presents no arguments against Dibelius's evidence but only, quite correctly, shows that Dibelius was involved in a logical inconsistency in ruling out a direct reference, in James 2:14 ff., to Rom. 4. Dibelius's argument, simply put, is that James cannot refer to Paul because the faith caricatured and the works advocated in James are so different from what Paul really meant by faith and works;[48] yet Dibelius almost immediately notes that "it was indeed the fate of Paul to be mis-

45. Eichholz, *Jakobus und Paulus*, p. 40.

46. Dibelius, *Brief des Jakobus*, p. 221.

47. Cf. Dibelius's excursus on "The Abraham Example," in *Brief des Jakobus*, pp. 206–14, and the summary of the differences, p. 220, n. 2; also Windisch, *Die katholischen Briefe*, p. 21. The argument of Bo Reicke, *The Epistles of James, Peter, and Jude*, p. 5, that James 2:14 ff. does not have Paul in mind because Paul is not mentioned, is extremely weak.

48. Dibelius, *Brief des Jakobus*, p. 219. One should note that the same evidence may be advanced in support of the argument for *early* authorship of James. Cf. Gerhard Kittel, "Der geschichtliche Ort des Jakobusbriefes," *ZNW* 41 (1942): 102.

understood in the Church."[49] Eichholz rests content, however,[50] with showing that Dibelius has himself undercut the argument that James cannot be referring directly to Paul's writings since one could simply say that James is a case in the point that Paul was misunderstood. Rather than advancing any new evidence to prove the contrary, Eichholz moves instead into an attempt to show that Paul and James can be reconciled, at least to a great degree, by understanding the two authors to share a theology of obedience to the Word. This Word of God, spoken into different situations, necessitates emphases' falling in different places. James and Paul are not, therefore, in conflict with each other, and the theological unity of the canon is preserved.[51]

While that issue does not concern us here, we are interested in discovering what, if any, principles guided James's selection of certain paraenetic materials. Thus it is important to know whether the author of James really had Rom. 4 in mind when he wrote James 2:14 ff.; that is, if it can be determined more exactly what the position is against which James argues, perhaps one can more readily discover any ethical principles that may be underlying the argument. It does, in fact, seem possible to demonstrate that James 2:14 ff. actually seeks deliberately to counter Rom. 3 f. It is not necessary to make any attempt to discredit the evidence marshalled by Dibelius, in his excursus on "The Abraham Example,"[52] for the purpose of showing that the paraenetic use of Abraham as an example of faith belongs within a Jewish tradition of interpretation. That will certainly stand, and Paul's own use of the example of Abraham doubtless also draws from this tradition.[53] What Dibelius (and others) seem to have overlooked, however, is the

49. Dibelius, *Brief des Jakobus*, p. 221.

50. Eichholz, *Jakobus und Paulus*, p. 41.

51. Eichholz begins to develop this position toward the end of *Jakobus und Paulus*, and it is then the central issue of *Glaube und Werke*. Cf. especially *Jakobus und Paulus*, p. 46, and *Glaube und Werke*, pp. 40–45.

52. Dibelius, *Brief des Jakobus*, pp. 206–14. Roy Bowen Ward, "The Works of Abraham," *HarvTheolRev* 61 (1968): 283–90, tries to go beyond Dibelius's position by showing that Abraham's justification in James is related to his famous hospitality, which eventuated in his being known as "friend of God." Thus James would appear to represent a unique development of the Jewish tradition about Abraham, and it would be further unnecessary to relate the Abraham example in James to Paul. But James must be related to Paul at this point, as the following evidence demonstrates.

53. So also Dibelius, *Brief des Jakobus*, p. 215.

way in which the language about faith in the context of the Abraham example in James parallels the language about faith in the context of the Abraham example in Romans but reverses it. The opposition of faith and works, of course, in both places is what calls forth such attempts at explanation as those of Dibelius and Eichholz; but the statement that seems to settle the matter is James 2:24: "Man is justified by works [*ex ergōn*] and not by faith [*ek pisteōs*] alone [*monon*]." The phrase *ek pisteōs* occurs, however, in this sense nowhere in the whole literature of early Christianity outside Romans, Galatians, and James![54] Its use in James 2:24 can therefore hardly be considered accidental. The phrase "by faith alone [*ek pisteōs monon*]," however, which sounds very much like something Paul would have written, actually never occurs in any of Paul's writings.[55] The use of *monon* in James 2:24 of course has its explanation in James's argument, i.e., James is not denying the validity of faith, he is only denying the validity of faith that cannot be demonstrated by works;[56] but his choice of phraseology here is also determined by Rom. 3 and 4. Paul had written in Rom. 4:16, in a way that almost defies translation, "On account of this [sc., the way in which the law effected wrath, v. 15], [righteousness is] by faith [*ek pisteōs*], in order [that it may be a righteousness] of grace [*kata charin*], for the promise to all the seed to be fixed, not *only* to the [seed] of the law [*ou tōi ek tou nomou monon*] but also to the [seed] *of* Abraham's *faith* [*tōi ek pisteōs Abraam*]." Furthermore, Paul had quoted Ps. 143:2 in Rom. 3:20, prefixing to it the words "by works of the law [*ex ergōn nomou*]": "By works of the law no flesh is justified before him"; and he had then rephrased this in his own words: "We consider man to be justified by faith apart from works of the law" (Rom. 3:28; contrast James 2:24: "You see that man is justified by works and not by faith alone"). James 2:24 thus appears to be a conscious attempt to reverse the Pauline language of Rom. 3:28,

54. Precisely, *ek pisteōs* occurs twelve times in Romans (once in the quotation of Hab. 2:4), eight times in Galatians (again once in the quotation of Hab. 2:4), in Heb. 10:38 (only in the quotation of Hab. 2:4), in Hermas Visiones iii, 8, 7 in the statement, "self-control is born out of faith," and in James 2:24.

55. *Pace* Dan Otto Via, Jr., "The Right Strawy Epistle Reconsidered," p. 257, who states, apparently without having consulted a concordance, that *ek pisteōs monon* is found only in James *and* Paul.

56. Dibelius, *Brief des Jakobus*, pp. 191–95, 218 f., offers a thorough discussion of this point.

whereby language from Rom. 4:16 is also brought in. The "law" of Rom. 3:28 has fallen out, so that James has only "by works [*ex ergōn*]"; and Paul's qualification on Abraham's biological descendants, *ou tōi ek tou nomou monon* (Rom. 4:16), has suggested to the author of James a reverse use of the word *monon* (whereby he of course misses Paul's meaning in Rom. 4:16), so that he now asserts that man is not justified by faith *alone* (James 2:24).

In other words, Paul's statement in Rom. 3:28, "We consider man to be justified by faith apart from works of the law," is a paraphrase of Ps. 143:2, which Paul had quoted in verse 20. Rom. 3:28 is therefore related to the example of Abraham only because they both belong to Paul's argument. The relationship of Ps. 143:2, paraphrased in Rom. 3:28, to the Abraham example cannot be derived from the Jewish tradition about Abraham as an example, and therefore the only tie between James's use of the Abraham example and his statement in 2:24 is Rom. 3:28. Had the author of James not read Rom. 3 f., the language of James 2:24 would not have suggested itself to him merely out of the tradition of the interpretation about Abraham.[57]

When such use of Pauline language occurs precisely in a discussion of the relative value of faith and works for justification, and when Abraham is also adduced as the example par excellence, there can hardly be any doubt that we have to do here with much more than the coincidence brought about by common reliance on Jewish tradition that found in Abraham the example par excellence of the work of faith. We have to do rather with a conscious and deliberate attempt to reverse the argument of Paul in Rom. 3 f.[58] The question is, why?

James himself will have to tell us. Let us agree at the outset that he misunderstands Paul. He exchanges works of the law for the good deeds done by a Christian, and he separates faith as something distinct from those Christian deeds, something that

57. It is this point which, it seems to me, bests the argument of Dibelius, *Brief des Jakobus*, pp. 203, 211, that the conclusive proof that James relies on Jewish tradition is to be found in James 2:23, where Gen. 15:6 is quoted and referred to justification by works. I do not mean that this point is to be denied, but rather that it is penultimate in view of the reliance of James 2:24 on Rom. 3:28. Dibelius, *Brief des Jakobus*, p. 204, devotes only seven lines to James 2:24!

58. So also Kurt Aland, "Der Herrenbruder Jakobus und der Jakobusbrief," *ThLZ* 69 (1944): 104.

Paul would not have done (cf. his imperative in the indicative). In misunderstanding Paul, James is not alone, since Paul's own followers (the authors of the deutero-Pauline Epistles and 1 Peter) did not understand him, and Dibelius has already explained that "it was indeed the fate of Paul to be misunderstood in the Church."[59] But how *did* James understand Paul—that is, what was the nature of his misunderstanding? On this we are already fully informed. James's understanding of what Paul meant by faith *apart from works* was a faith that could ignore works, that could say to a fellow Christian (brother or sister, James 2:15) who was naked or starving, "Go in peace, be warmed and fed" (v. 15), without doing anything to alleviate the cold or the hunger. To this he adds (v. 17), in the event that the reader has missed his killing sarcasm, that such a faith is dead. But that means that, for James, *Paul's* faith is dead! James is thus willing to oppose what is fast becoming, if it is not already, holy tradition—the writings of Paul.[60] The like is not to be found, to my knowledge, elsewhere in early Christianity. The author of 2 Peter may declare (2 Pet. 3:16) that Paul's letters contain "certain things difficult to understand," but that is about as far as an early Christian seems to have been willing to go in the direction of the rejection of written tradition. Elsewhere, the technique seems to have been, following rabbinic practice, to interpret the tradition so that it would come out where one wished. Not so James. He rejects the tradition. He turns its own language and proof texts back upon it and reverses its intent. There can be no doubt that he does this for a principle —and it will have to be a principle of supreme importance to have led him so deliberately and bluntly to oppose emerging holy tradition—and the question therefore becomes whether that principle can be discerned.

J. B. Souček finds the principle in the intent of James to turn the congregation away from emerging "internalizing, individualizing, and also theoretizing" toward a "solidarity of life in the congregation . . . in which no one in need would have to stand

---

59. Dibelius, *Brief des Jakobus*, p. 221.

60. J. B. Souček, "Zu den Problemen des Jakobusbriefes," *EvTh* 18 (1958): 468, refers to "sanctified Pauline statements."

alone."[61] This, he thinks, is the point of James's several attacks on the rich. It is not that James means to exclude the rich from the congregation, but he wants them to take their "rightful," that is "even lowly place."[62] Thus the point of 2:14 ff. is that the *rich* in the congregation cannot escape their obligations to the poor Christians, and the argument of 2:10 f., that the one who transgresses one of the commandments has transgressed them all, therefore means, in the context of verse 9 (it is a transgression to make distinctions of personal worth), that the rich man who does not care properly for the poor is as guilty as a murderer.[63] Thus James has dared to oppose the holy tradition of the writings of Paul "in order to move against the danger of replacing the brotherly congregation by an abstractly and theoretically constructed and individualistically narrowed piety."[64]

A somewhat similar approach has been taken by Dan O. Via, Jr., who suggests that James "wants to maintain that Christian faith calls for an attitude of love and for concrete deeds, and he also wants to break through legalism. But he does not do the latter consistently or successfully."[65] Too easily, however, Via assumes that James's citation of the love commandment in 2:8, which James calls the "royal law," provides us with James's definition of law *as such*, especially in the subsequent discussion of individual commandments; and he also too easily assumes that the good deeds of 2:14 ff. are "deeds of neighborly *love*."[66] Both assumptions are open to question.

Surely Dibelius is wrong when he argues that "we have no cause

---

61. Ibid., p. 466. In addition, Souček also finds the testing of faith to be a theme in James, but that is unrelated to our interest here.
62. Ibid., p. 464. Johannes Leipoldt, *Der soziale Gedanke in der altchristlichen Kirche*, p. 138, takes the extreme view: the poor are "God's darlings; he damns the rich."
63. Souček, *Problemen des Jakobusbriefes*, p. 465.
64. Ibid., p. 468. Dibelius also takes into consideration a definite "piety of poverty" (*Armenfrömmigkeit*) for James, only he does not find this to be a principle underlying the paraenesis as such. Cf. Dibelius, *Brief des Jakobus*, pp. 58–66, 70–73.
65. Via, "Right Strawy Epistle Reconsidered," p. 262. Reicke, *Epistles of James, Peter, and Jude*, p. 7, takes the "lack of system" in James to be only "apparent," suggesting that the true order is related to "the conditions current in the communities." The connection, however, between a Christianity in need of manifold advice and an epistle having no logical sequence escapes me.
66. Via, "Right Strawy Epistle Reconsidered," p. 256.

to relate *nomos basilikos* [royal law] to the love commandment,"
and that James's quotation of that commandment in 2:8 is unrelated to the famous saying of Jesus.[67] That the royal law is the
love commandment is what James says in 2:8 about as explicitly
as possible, and Windisch suggests that the term *royal* law is applied here either because it is the law given by the king (whether
God or Jesus would thereby be meant he does not discuss) or because of the "surpassing significance of this commandment" in
Christianity.[68] There seems to be no evidence that would conclu-
sively prove that James here cites the saying of the Lord, but, after
all the evidence we have seen in this study of the tenacious way in
which the love commandment maintains some place, however
small, in the ethical traditions of the New Testament, it has to be
seen as unlikely that a Christian writer of the second generation
could not know that the love commandment belonged to the
bedrock of Christian tradition. But Via's assumption that James
defines law as the law of love is also mistaken. Here, Dibelius's
observation that the love commandment appears as "one alongside others—for otherwise the proof adduced in vv. 10 f. would
have no meaning" is more correct,[69] although perhaps it is most
true to James 2:8 ff. to say that the love commandment *formally*
occupies a place of superior rank (mentioned first and separately,
designated royal law) but that it *materially* stands only as one
commandment among others. James's use of the love commandment, then, reminds us of the use of *agapē* in Colossians.

Also, it appears to be an overly hasty conclusion on Via's part
to consider the proper treatment of the needy, in 2:14 ff., to be
subsumed under the love commandment. The love commandment
falls entirely out of the picture after 2:9. It is verse 9, in fact,
which gives the best explanation of what our author means by
agapē: not making distinctions regarding personal worth[70]—that
is, treating everyone equally, or perhaps appropriately; but there

67. Dibelius, *Brief des Jakobus*, p. 177. So also Victor Paul Furnish, *The Love
Command in the New Testament*, pp. 177–80.

68. Windisch, *Die katholischen Briefe*, p. 15.

69. Dibelius, *Brief des Jakobus*, p. 177. Windisch, *Die katholischen Briefe*, p. 12,
thinks that the "religious and moral commandments" (not the whole Torah) are
"subordinated" to "faith, righteousness, love." I cannot see the evidence for this.

70. So also Windisch, *Die katholischen Briefe*, p. 15.

is no indication at all in 2:14 ff. that it is the love commandment that has led James to reject the faith that fails to care for the needy.

If not the love commandment, then what? Via seems to be correct that James wants "to break through legalism," but what leads James to attempt this break? The emphasizing, in 2:11, that the person who has broken *one* law has broken *the law* establishes Via's "inconsistently and unsuccessfully," since James here wants to get around a petty and ridiculous legalism that takes pride in keeping certain laws; yet he retains the validity of the law. The line of argument in 2:14–26, however, is unrelated to this; rather, James here takes up another matter, the problem of those who (in his understanding), like Paul, pride themselves on their faith.[71] To boast about one's faith, explains James, is wrong as long as that faith does not produce works, certain works. Why precisely these works? If James does not arrive at the examples of feeding and clothing fellow Christians who are needy on the basis of the love commandment (Via), neither does he do so on the principle that the rich must care for the poor in the interest of the solidarity of the congregation (Souček). The principles of the organization of the paraenesis lead to the conclusion that such a possibility, just as in the case of the love commandment, is also to be ruled out. The only possibilities left are that James's choice of "works" to be evaluated positively is arbitrary or that something about the discussion of faith and works leads him to think of certain works. Since it can be demonstrated that James's discussion of faith and works rests on Rom. 3 f., and since that passage speaks rather of works of law, the second possibility is unlikely, and we are left with caring for the needy as an arbitrary example of the test of faith.

Beyond this, one can make only the most cautious assumptions, but it would seem that, if James's example is arbitrary, then such "works" were merely obvious to him at face value—that is, not to

---

71. What leads James from the issue of 2:10–13 to that of 2:14 ff. is the common denominator of laying emphasis on the wrong thing—in 2:10–13 on not breaking certain laws, in 2:14 ff. on having faith. This explanation follows the rules of connection between adjacent items in the paraenesis explained by Dibelius, *Brief des Jakobus*, pp. 21–23, although Dibelius declares, regarding 2:14 ff., that "a connection with the preceding discussion is not to be suggested" (*Brief des Jakobus*, p. 184).

care for the needy would not be human (or, since we have to do only with needy Christians, not Christian, but without any prior principle establishing the "Christianity" of such caring, i.e., not Christian because not human). If that assumption however, appears at all likely, then we have come to a most important new point in New Testament ethics, for nowhere else in the New Testament has that principle and that principle alone determined ethical advice. We have seen, it is true, in the deutero-Pauline literature a tendency, in some cases quite pronounced, to define Christian ethics as the standards of good citizenship. Here, however, is something more basic, mere humanity. I am suggesting that the most likely explanation for James's example of the works faith should produce is the emergence here of a humanistic principle, the principle that human beings should be dealt with humanely and that this principle does not rest on any prior ethical or theological *principle* but that it rather breaks in here, or, better, "crops up." There is no evidence of any prior principle at work in the selection of the example; rather, when James looks around to see what one would do to attest one's faith, what he comes up with is a humane response to basic human need.[72]

To be sure, James has only Christians ("a brother or a sister," 2:15) in mind, and not everyone. As Via says, "He does not [break through legalism] consistently or successfully"; perhaps he would not have understood the importance that is here being attached to his example. He makes no move in the direction of systematizing his position, for the Epistle of James remains, after all, a paraenetic tract, just as Dibelius has described it. Something im-

72. This does not mean that the ultimate origin of James's humane response cannot be known; it is doubtless a Jewish commonplace. Windisch, *Die katholischen Briefe*, p. 17, refers to Isa. 58:6 f.; Testament of Zebulon 7:1–3; Testament of Issachar 7:5; and Matt. 25:34 ff. These indeed provide close parallels (e.g., Testament of Issachar: "I sighed with every person in pain, and I divided my bread with the poor"), but such a concern for basic human need is as old as Israelite religion itself. Already the Covenant Code (Exod. 22:26 f., RSV) requires that "if ever you take your neighbor's garment in pledge, you shall restore it to him before the sun goes down; for that is his only covering, it is his mantle for his body; in what else shall he sleep?" Amos 5:12 chastises those who "turn aside the needy in the gate" (RSV), and Prov. 25:21 advises, "If your enemy is hungry, give him bread to eat; and if he is thirsty, give him water to drink" (RSV). Cf. further the comments of Bousset in Wilhelm Bousset, *Die Religion des Judentums im späthellenistischen Zeitalter*, ed. Hugo Gressmann, HNT, 21 (Tübingen, 1925³; reprint ed., 1966⁴). James's Jewish rearing or conditioning had surely provided him with the viewpoint which he here expresses in the nature of something that he takes for granted.

portant has nevertheless happened here; a Christian has turned against his Christian tradition for the sake of his fellow man.

One might wish to carry the concern for the fellow Christian expressed here in James back to Christian tradition, to argue that we here have tradition played off against tradition, the tradition of, say, the good Samaritan played off against Paul. Although it is possible that the feeding and clothing of needy Christians turns up here as one stage of a part of the Christian tradition, and not as only a commonsense commonplace, that is not demonstrable. The literary analysis of James and the way in which the concern for the needy is formulated here without justification—but only in contrast to faith without works—prevent such a demonstration. The only conclusion that one can draw about the origin of such concern expressed in this passage, based on James itself, is that it arises out of the author's general, probably Jewish heritage.

It would have been nice had the author of James elsewhere brought the same humanistic principle into play, but such evidence is found only with difficulty, or even not at all. The only other passage in James that seems in any way to suggest itself is 1:13–15, where it is denied that God tempts anyone to evil, and the author argues that, instead, one's own desires [*hē epithymia*] bring about sin. This idea, which is at least as old as Homer,[73] represents a humanistic tendency, since it maintains that a major sphere of human existence, human misfortune, is caused, not by the gods, but by men. James in no way relates this concept to ethics, however, but rather uses it as a stepping-stone toward the assertion (1:16–18) that all good things come from God. There is certainly no connection between these verses and 2:14 ff.

We are therefore left only with the arbitrarily brought in humanism of 2:15 f., which disappears as suddenly as it appears; we must not attribute to our author more than the evidence allows! Nevertheless, he has made a most interesting and original, perhaps even daring move, although he makes no attempt to consolidate the humanistic position. The Christian, however, who wishes to

---

73. Cf. Homer, *Odyssey* 1. 32–34 (Zeus speaks): "What a lamentable thing it is that men should blame the gods and regard *us* as the source of their troubles, when it is their own wickedness that brings them sufferings worse than any which Destiny allots them" (trans. E. V. Rieu [Baltimore, 1946]). Dibelius, *Brief des Jakobus*, pp. 121–25, also attests extensive Hellenistic Jewish parallels.

find within the New Testament some ethical guidance that is valid today will be grateful that James is a part of the canon.[74]

There is, finally, no consistent principle or set of principles upon which James relies for his paraenesis. The principles are as varied as the injunctions and are unrelated to one another (except that James does indeed seem to have a dislike for and distrust of wealthy persons). Other than the humanitarianism all too briefly glimpsed, James provides nothing upon which one could rely or to which one could appeal for ethics today—although one may certainly agree or disagree with individual positions taken in James; but such agreement or disagreement will invariably be on the basis of other criteria.

74. This, of course, is also the position of Eichholz; cf. *Glaube und Werke*, p. 44. The differences lie, however, in the manner of arriving at the position and in the implications drawn from it.

EPILOGUE

It may be that some readers, having arrived at this point, are disappointed, having expected something more. A few may wonder whether a study having such overwhelmingly negative conclusions should have been carried through to completion. One hopes, however, that the forest has not hidden the trees; for the conclusions were not uniform. Among the "non-negative" findings in the study were Luke's admittedly unexciting alteration of the love commandment into a "good Samaritan" norm, James's visceral humane reaction against what he took to be inhumane ascending Christian theology, and Paul's fleeting denial of eschatology in favor of the *qualitative transcendence* of love. Surely the latter two of these New Testament perspectives are overdue for discussion in the church and among other persons who are willing to grant some kind of normative validity to the New Testament.

Will theologians continue to ignore James because he opposes Paul, who—every theologian knows—is normative a priori? Will ethicists continue to publish still more works predicated on the false assumption that the command to love is some kind of norm or middle axiom laid down as a law that is valid for all times? (a notion which this study should lay to rest, although I have no false hopes). Can theologians and philosophers reflect (a few are still able) on the validity of the concept of qualitatively transcendent love and the implications of such a notion? These would appear to be the alternatives remaining. Otherwise, throw out the New Testament as an aid to ethics once and for all.

It is of course true that the conclusions are, indeed, overwhelmingly negative; but studies in controversial areas should not be undertaken—or published—only when they are affirmative! It is instructive at this point to return to Albert Schweitzer's *Quest of the Historical Jesus* and to recall some of his concluding remarks. "Those who are fond of talking about negative theology," he stated at the outset of his concluding chapter, "can find their account here. There is nothing more negative than" his study.[1] A few sentences later he observed that, "whatever the ultimate solution may be, the historical Jesus of whom the criticism of the future . . . will draw the portrait, can never render modern theology the services which it claimed from its own half-historical, half-modern, Jesus." Finally, "we must be prepared to find that the historical knowledge of the personality and life of Jesus will not be a help, but perhaps even an offense to religion."[2]

So it is with the study of New Testament ethics. The ethical positions of the New Testament are the children of their own times and places, alien and foreign to this day and age. Amidst the ethical dilemmas which confront us, we are now at least relieved of the need or temptation to begin with Jesus, or the early church, or the New Testament, if we wish to develop coherent ethical positions. We are freed from bondage to that tradition, and we are able to propose, with the author of the Epistle of James, that tradition and precedent must not be allowed to stand in the way of what is humane and right.

If this study thus succeeds in arousing among its readers a (perhaps renewed) intellectual examination of our ethical traditions and of the New Testament material, if it succeeds in creating even some new direction in studies in those areas, it will have accomplished its purpose.

It is tempting, in concluding, to make a comprehensive statement—to indicate how, at least in outline, a valid ethics for here and now may be developed. I resist the temptation. That is a topic for discussion elsewhere, and doubtless by others.

1. Albert Schweitzer, *The Quest of the Historical Jesus*, p. 396.
2. Ibid., p. 399.

BIBLIOGRAPHY

BIBLIOGRAPHY

Barrett, C. K. *A Commentary on the Epistle to the Romans.* Harper's New Testament Commentaries. New York, 1957.

————. *The Gospel According to St. John.* London, 1955.

Barth, Karl. *The Resurrection of the Dead.* Translated by H. J. Stenning. New York, 1933.

Beare, Francis W. "The Epistle to the Colossians: Introduction and Exegesis." In *The Interpreter's Bible.* Vol. 11. Edited by George A. Buttrick. New York and Nashville, 1955.

Bornkamm, Günther. *Jesus of Nazareth.* Translated by Irene and Fraser McLuskey with James M. Robinson. London, 1960.

————, Gerhard Barth, and Heinz Joachim Held. *Tradition and Interpretation in Matthew.* Translated by Percy Scott. The New Testament Library. Philadelphia, 1963.

Braun, Herbert. *Jesus: Der Mann aus Nazareth und seine Zeit.* Themen der Theologie, 1. Stuttgart-Berlin, 1969.

————. "The Problem of a New Testament Theology." Translated by Jack T. Sanders. *JThC* 1 (1965).

Brown, Raymond E. *The Gospel According to John (xiii–xxi).* The Anchor Bible. Garden City, N.Y., 1970.

Brown, Schuyler. *Apostasy and Perseverance in the Theology of Luke.* Analecta Biblica, 36. Rome, 1969.

Bultmann, Rudolf. *The Gospel of John: A Commentary.* Translated by G. R. Beasley-Murray. Oxford, 1971.

————. *The History of the Synoptic Tradition.* Translated by John Marsh. New York and Evanston, 1963.

————. *Jesus and the Word.* Translated by Louise Pettibone Smith and Erminie Huntress Lantero. New York, 1934.

————. *The Johannine Epistles.* Translated by R. Philip O'Hara with Lane C. McGaughy and Robert W. Funk. Hermeneia. Philadelphia, 1973.

————. *Theology of the New Testament.* 2 vols. Translated by Kendrick Grobel. New York, 1951, 1955.

Cadbury, Henry J. *The Making of Luke-Acts.* London, 1927.

————. *The Peril of Modernizing Jesus.* New York, 1937.

Campenhausen, Hans von. "Zur Auslegung von Röm 13: Die dämonistische Deutung des EXOUSIA-Begriffs." In *Festschrift Alfred Bertholet zum 80. Geburtstag.* Tübingen, 1950.

Conzelmann, Hans. *An Outline of the Theology of the New Testament.* Translated by John Bowden. New York and Evanston, 1969.

——. *Der erste Brief an die Korinther.* Kritisch-exegetischer Kommentar über das Neue Testament. Göttingen, 1969[11]. Cf. the forthcoming English translation in the Hermeneia series.

——. *The Theology of St Luke.* Translated by Geoffrey Buswell. New York, 1960.

Dibelius, Martin. *An die Kolosser Epheser an Philemon.* Neu bearbeitet von Heinrich Greeven. HNT, 12. Tübingen, 1953[3].

——. *Der Brief des Jakobus.* Herausgegeben und ergänzt von Heinrich Greeven. Kritisch-exegetischer Kommentar über das Neue Testament. Göttingen, 1964[11]. (First published in 1921.) Cf. the forthcoming English translation in the Hermeneia series.

Dodd, C. H. *The Interpretation of the Fourth Gospel.* Cambridge: 1953.

——. *The Parables of the Kingdom.* Rev. ed. New York, 1961.

Easton, Burton Scott. "New Testament Ethical Lists." *JBL* 51 (1932).

Eichholz, Georg. *Glaube und Werke bei Paulus und Jakobus.* Theologische Existenz heute, N.F. 88. Munich, 1961.

——. *Jakobus und Paulus: Ein Beitrag zum Problem des Kanons.* Theologische Existenz heute, N.F. 39. Munich, 1953.

Feuillet, André. *Johannine Studies.* Translated by Thomas E. Crane. Staten Island, N.Y., 1965.

Fuchs, Ernst. "Glaube und Geschichte im Blick auf die Frage nach dem historischen Jesus (Zu G. Bornkamms Buch über Jesus von Nazareth)." In *Zur Frage nach dem historischen Jesus.* Tübingen, 1960.

——. "Was heisst: 'Du sollst deinen Nächsten lieben wie dich selbst'?" In *Zur Frage nach dem historischen Jesus.* Tübingen, 1960.

Funk, Robert W. *Language, Hermeneutic, and Word of God: The Problem of Language in the New Testament and Contemporary Theology.* New York, Evanston, and London, 1966.

Furnish, Victor Paul. *The Love Command in the New Testament.* Nashville and New York, 1972.

——. *Theology and Ethics in Paul.* Nashville and New York, 1968.

Hiers, Richard H. *The Kingdom of God in the Synoptic Tradition.* University of Florida Humanities Monographs, 33. Gainesville, Fla., 1970.

Käsemann, Ernst. *New Testament Questions of Today.* Translated by W. J. Montague. Philadelphia, 1969.

——. *The Testament of Jesus: A Study of the Gospel of John in the Light of Chapter 17.* Translated by Gerhard Krodel. Philadelphia, 1968.

——. *Das wandernde Gottesvolk: Eine Untersuchung zum Hebräerbrief.* FRLANT, N.F. 37. Göttingen, 1961[4].

Kelly, J. N. D. *A Commentary on the Epistles of Peter and Jude.*
Black's New Testament Commentaries. London, 1969.

Kümmel, Werner Georg. *Introduction to the New Testament.* Founded
by Paul Feine and Johannes Behm. Translated by A. J. Mattill, Jr.
Nashville and New York, 1966[14].

Kuhl, Josef, SVD. *Die Sendung Jesu und der Kirche nach dem Johannes-Evangelium.* Studia Instituti Missiologici Societatis Verbi Divini,
11. St. Augustin/Siegburg, 1967.

Leipoldt, Johannes. *Der soziale Gedanke in der altchristlichen Kirche.*
Leipzig, 1952.

Lippert, Peter. *Leben als Zeugnis.* Stuttgarter Biblische Monographien,
4. Stuttgart, 1968.

Lohmeyer, Ernst. *Das Evangelium des Markus.* Kritisch-exegetischer
Kommentar über das Neue Testament. Göttingen, 1963[16].

Lohse, Eduard. *Colossians and Philemon.* Edited by Helmut Koester.
Translated by William R. Poehlmann and Robert J. Karris. Hermeneia. Philadelphia, 1971.

Merk, Otto. *Handeln aus Glauben: Die Motivierung der paulinischen
Ethik.* Marburger theologische Studien, 5. Marburg, 1968.

Meyer, Arnold. *Das Rätsel des Jacobusbriefes.* BZNW, 10. Giessen,
1930.

Michel, Otto. *Der Brief an die Hebräer.* Kritisch-exegetischer Kommentar über das Neue Testament. Göttingen, 1966[12].

―――. *Der Brief an die Römer.* Kritisch-exegetischer Kommentar
über das Neue Testament. Göttingen, 1963[12].

Moffatt, James. *A Critical and Exegetical Commentary on the Epistle
to the Hebrews.* I.C.C. Edinburgh, 1924.

Perrin, Norman. *Rediscovering the Teaching of Jesus.* New York and
Evanston, 1967.

Preisker, Herbert. *Das Ethos des Urchristentums.* Darmstadt, 1968[3].
(First published in 1933.)

Reicke, Bo. *The Epistles of James, Peter, and Jude.* The Anchor Bible.
Garden City, N.Y., 1964.

Robinson, James M. *A New Quest of the Historical Jesus.* SBT, 25.
Naperville, Ill. 1959.

Sanders, Jack T. "First Corinthians 13: Its Interpretation Since the
First World War." *Interpretation* 20 (1966).

Schweitzer, Albert. *The Kingdom of God and Primitive Christianity.*
Edited by Ulrich Neuenschwander. Translated by L. A. Garrard.
New York, 1968.

―――. *The Quest of the Historical Jesus: A Critical Study of Its
Progress from Reimarus to Wrede.* Translated by W. Montgomery.
London, 1954.

Schweizer, Eduard. *The Good News According to Mark.* Translated
by Donald H. Madvig. Richmond, Va., 1970.

Selwyn, Edward Gordon. *The First Epistle of St. Peter.* London, 1955.
Souček, J. B. "Zu den Problemen des Jakobusbriefes." *EvTh* 18 (1958).
Spicq, C. *L'Épître aux Hébreux,* 2 vols. Études bibliques. Paris, 1952³, 1953.
————. *Saint Paul: Les Épîtres pastorales,* 2 vols. Études bibliques. Paris, 1969⁴.
Strecker, Georg. *Der Weg der Gerechtigkeit: Untersuchung zur Theologie des Matthäus.* FRLANT, 82. Göttingen, 1962.
Tannehill, Robert C. *Dying and Rising with Christ: A Study in Pauline Theology.* BZNW, 32. Berlin, 1967.
Theissen, Gerd. *Untersuchungen zum Hebräerbrief.* Studien zum Neuen Testament, 2. Gütersloh, 1969.
Via, Dan Otto, Jr. "The Right Strawy Epistle Reconsidered: A Study in Biblical Ethics and Hermeneutic." *JR* 49 (1969).
Weidinger, Karl. *Die Haustafeln: Ein Stück urchristlicher Paränese.* Untersuchungen zum Neuen Testament, 14. Leipzig, 1928.
Wendland, Heinz-Dietrich. *Ethik des Neuen Testaments: Eine Einführung.* Das Neue Testament Deutsch: Ergänzungsreihe, 4. Göttingen, 1970.
Wibbing, Siegfried. *Die Tugend- und Lasterkataloge im Neuen Testament und ihre Traditionsgeschichte unter besonderer Berücksichtigung der Qumran-Texte.* BZNW, 25. Berlin, 1959.
Wilder, Amos N. *Eschatology and Ethics in the Teaching of Jesus.* Rev. ed. New York, 1950.
Windisch, Hans. *Die katholischen Briefe.* HNT, 15. Tübingen, 1930².

INDEXES

INDEX OF BIBLICAL REFERENCES

(See also the table of contents)

INDEX OF MODERN AUTHORS